OLD TESTAMENT GUIDES

General Editor

R.N. Whybray

JOB

JOB

J. H. Eaton

Published by JSOT Press
for the Society for Old Testament Study

In memory of Ted and Ernie,
two kind-hearted Cornish brothers

Copyright © 1985 JSOT Press

Published by
JSOT Press
Department of Biblical Studies
The University of Sheffield
Sheffield S10 2TN
England

Photoset and Printed in Great Britain
by Redwood Burn Limited,
Trowbridge, Wiltshire.

British Library Cataloguing in Publication Data

Eaton, J.H.
Job.—(Old Testament guides, ISSN 0264–6498; 5)
1. Bible—O.T. Job—Commentaries
I. Title II. Series
223'.106   BS1415.3

ISBN 0–905774–97–3

CONTENTS

Chapter 2

Gathering our Observations: Structure and Theme

Chapter 3

Questions of Context and Language

PREFACE

IT WILL BE SEEN that I have composed this 'Guide' with the primary aim of assisting a careful and appreciative reading of *Job*. Discussion of the questions that arise in our minds is then developed on the basis of the facts that we have seen for ourselves. With our own experience of the main data, we can enjoy debating the issues and can take a genuine interest in the differing judgments of scholars. Such is the greatness of *Job*, that no one is likely to regret effort spent first on the appreciative encounter I am advocating.

The same principle applies to my account of the comparable literature from the ancient world. Those who take the texts in their own hands will have the most satisfaction, wondering that in so many lands and from such ancient times the meaning of life has been so eloquently debated.

Since translation and exegesis are part of one work, I have preferred to give my occasional quotations from *Job* in my own translation. I hope it will sometimes supplement the impression of the original poetry which the reader gains from the English version of his choice (cf. pp. 64–65).

I am most grateful to Professor R.N. Whybray for his careful work as General Editor, resulting in many improvements. All books should have such an editor.

University of Birmingham, August 1984   J.H. Eaton

INTRODUCTION

T HE BOOK OF JOB leads us by story and poetry through the depths and heights of human experience. By story and poetry that take the form of a drama we are involved in the greatest of all human struggles: to see the world's evil honestly and still believe in good.

Our poet's gifts of expression match the intensity of his feelings and vision. There is general agreement that his work stands at the summit of Hebrew literature and among the world's great masterpieces. The likelihood is that those who get to know it well, and so participate in its drama, will not vastly differ from the judgment of that great Scottish man of letters, Thomas Carlyle, in his *On Heroes*: 'One of the grandest things ever written ... There is nothing written, I think, in the Bible or out of it, of equal literary merit.'

To the student it offers also much challenge. The course of the drama takes surprising turns, and at times we wonder whether the paradoxes are the intention of the author or the products of the book's later history. To turn straight to the scholarly debate on these questions is to court mental indigestion, so many are the permutations that have been suggested. The sound course, therefore, is to read the Book of Job itself, with all attention and sympathy, and with only a restrained guide at one's elbow to help through difficult turning points and share first reactions. When one has thus gained direct knowledge of the material, one can enter into the discussion of critical questions with profit and enjoyment.

Chapter 1 of the present work is intended to accompany such a reading of *Job*. It marks out the sections of the text and underlines the main thoughts and their connections. Reading the text, part by part, with this running commentary to hand, one should readily appreciate the force of the story and poetry, and also the basic facts which constitute the chief problems.

In Chapter 2 the observations we have made are ordered and developed. First we treat the structural relation of the book's parts, and then the main ideas expressed in the parts and the whole.

In Chapter 3 we place the book in the context of other ancient literature that grappled with the meaning of life. It is a fascinating journey around western Asia, Africa, India and Greece. Further, we look into the poetic art of *Job* and the character of our English versions. We consider the time and place of the book's origin. And finally we glimpse *Job* in the context of the literature and studies it has evoked.

COMMENTARIES ON JOB

It will be convenient to list here a selection of commentaries, even if they remain in the background at this stage of our approach. The first five mentioned are the most suitable for those beginning biblical study.

D.J.A. Clines, 'Job', in *A Bible Commentary for Today*, ed. G.C.D. Howley, London and Glasgow: Pickering and Inglis, 1979, 559–92.

S. Terrien, 'Job', in *The Interpreter's Bible*, vol. 3, New York and Nashville: Abingdon Press, 1962, 877–1197.

A. and M. Hanson, *Job* (Torch Bible Commentaries), London: SCM Press, 1953.

N. Habel, *Job* (Cambridge Bible Commentary), London: Cambridge University Press, 1975.

F.I. Andersen, *Job* (Tyndale OT Commentaries), Leicester: Inter-Varsity Press, 1976. (Like the preceding works, suitable for beginners, but finding space for details and fresh judgments.)

H.H. Rowley, *Job* (New Century Bible), London: Nelson (later Oliphants), 1970. (This is notable for concise and balanced judgments and bird's eye views of scholarly debates.)

M.H. Pope, *Job* (Anchor Bible, 15), New York: Doubleday, 3rd edition 1973. (This has an emphasis on comparative material such as the texts from Ugarit.)

S.R. Driver and G.B. Gray, *Job* (International Critical Commentary), Edinburgh: T. & T. Clark, 1921. (This is a fundamental work, with much useful general material and also, gathered at the back, important philological notes.)

R. Gordis, *The Book of Job*, New York: Jewish Theological Seminary of America, 1978. (A large work especially useful for readers of the Hebrew text; note the sympathetic attitude to

Elihu, 546–53.)

E. Dhorme, *A Commentary on the Book of Job* (translated from the French original of 1926), London: Nelson, 1967. (This is highly esteemed for its clarity and thoroughness; the main commentary is an important discussion of the Hebrew text, but all can profit from the 224 pages of excellent introduction.)

Most of the above contain good lists of works on Job. The German contribution can be followed there through the names of Delitzsch, Hölscher, Weiser, Fohrer, and Horst. It will be convenient to add here two comprehensive discussions in German:

G. Fohrer, *Studien zum Buche Hiob (1956–1979)* (Beihefte zur *Zeitschrift für die alttestamentliche Wissenschaft*, 159), Berlin and New York: de Gruyter, 2nd edition 1983. (A collection of essays on various aspects of Job.)

V. Maag, *Hiob: Wandlung und Verarbeitung des Problems in Novelle, Dialogdichtung und Spätfussungen* (Forschungen zur Religion und Literatur des Alten und Neuen Testaments, 128), Göttingen: Vandenhoeck & Ruprecht, 1982. (A valuable discussion, though based on a complicated theory of sources and redactions.)

1

EXPERIENCING THE BOOK OF JOB: A GUIDED READING

The Prologue (chs 1–2)

BEFORE THE SPEECHES in poetry roll on their course of nearly forty chapters, we have the scene set for us by a master story-teller in two chapters of prose. It all happens in the land of Uz, which appears to be beyond Palestine on the fringes of the Syro-Arabian desert. Here lived the tribesmen of the Children of the East, with fields to plough, and camels, sheep and goats to graze. Among them, Job was the greatest. His devotion to God was genuine and complete, and from him God's blessing radiated on all his family and possessions. Thus his piety was matched by outstanding wealth, and he was ever-vigilant in devout observance to keep it so. Here, so far, we have an uncomplicated view of life under the just rule of God.

But swiftly the story brings a shadow into this rule. A conference gathers in heaven, a kind of annual assembly when the 'sons of God', who are his angelic servants, come before him to report and to hear his decisions. Among them is the Satan (which means 'the Adversary'), whose work is to patrol through the length and breadth of the earth evidently looking for faults to report for punishment. Because Job is so good—the best on earth, in the Lord's judgment—he becomes the subject of exchanges between the Lord and the Satan: 'You won't have found anything wrong with *him*!' But the Satan is accustomed to probe till he finds a fault. The outward appearance is good, but what of motivation? Job fears God, he suggests, to earn and keep his bountiful possessions. If God took those away, would he not curse him openly? God at once responds, authorizing the Satan to smite Job's possessions. The blows that come through the Satan, then, will represent the putting forth of God's own hand against Job to touch all that he has (1.11).

So we hear of the fateful day when four messengers come to Job in
turn, each arriving to report disaster while his predecessor is still
speaking. Thus swiftly he learns that he has lost his domestic animals, flocks, herds, servants, and children. But Job maintains his
piety. Tearing his robe in mourning, he bows low and blesses the
Lord who once gave and now has taken away.

In the account of the messengers we notice the story-teller's skill in
combining repetition and climax. And now, with the next meeting of
the heavenly assembly, we hear again repetition and fatal pro-
gression. The case of Job is again discussed. Of course Job will still
respect God, the persistent Satan suggests, for he still has himself to
protect. God now authorizes him to strike Job with disease, which re-
sults in sores from head to foot. What a fall from his dignity for the
greatest of all the Children of the East, as he sits now in mourning
outside the town on the mound of ashes and dung!

His behaviour is still pious. His wife would rather have him curse
God and so gain speedy death. 'Would you speak as one of the foolish
women?', he answers; 'Shall we accept good from God and not accept
bad?'

Some considerable time passes. The news reaches friendly digni-
taries of other tribes, who make appointment together and travel to
Job's side to mourn with him. There in traditional acts of sympathy
they weep and tear their robes and scatter dirt on their heads in
appeal to heaven, and sit beside him on the ground in silence for
seven days and nights.

The Prologue is ended. A skilful story indeed, but we may wonder
at what seems like crudity and harshness in the understanding of
God, traits which are in fact somewhat characteristic of the Old
Testament's colourful portrayals of God. The Lord (Hebrew
'Yahweh') is seen as the just ruler of the universe, rewarding good
and punishing wickedness, working through angelic servants; and
one of these servants can 'incite' or 'instigate' him (2.3) to launch an
appalling assault on the most blameless man, whom the Lord himself
has just singled out for highest praise, and so animals, servants and
children are violently slain for no fault of their own. All the same, the
story has achieved its dramatic purpose. We have been swept along to
the scene for the speeches: in a world ruled by a God intent on justice,
the most just of men has been placed, at God's decision, in an abyss of
protracted suffering, his happiness shattered by bereavement, disease and degradation.

Job and his Friends (chs 3–31)

Job's lamenting curse (ch. 3)
The long days of silence are ended abruptly. We hear Job expressing the misery of his condition in impassioned poetry. It is as though a saint had suddenly leapt from a stained glass window with rolling eyes and angry words. He does not curse God, but expresses his disgust at the gift of life by comprehensively cursing the day of his birth and the night of his conception. The days and nights of the year are thought of as a company of personal beings, each of which God seeks and calls to come forward in its annual turn. Job's curse would have his day and night of origin perish from the glad company, falling back into horrible darkness, because they did not stifle his life at the first.

He develops the wish that he had died at birth and unfolds envy and longing to be with the dead. In comparison with his present experience, the gloom of death has become in his eyes a blessed relief for all the oppressed company of mankind. He asks why life should be given to one in the extremes of misery, and portrays his state of groaning, fears continually realized, and ceaseless disquiet.

As we experience the fierce bitterness of this turning against life, we are struck also by its poetry. The first verse alone (3.1) would have sufficed for purposes of information. But beyond that we have a remarkable flow of poetic expression and imagery, as when we hear of the night which yearns towards daybreak, longing to look into the eyelids of dawn. Job's cursing of the day and night of his origins surely goes beyond the point of those psalm laments which sought to awaken the divine sympathy. As the passage reveals the bitterness of his experience with terrible beauty, we may wonder at the point of such ample poetry. Perhaps the answer lies in the need to communicate and to create from our deepest experience, even the bitterest.

Eliphaz's first speech (chs 4–5) and Job's reply (chs 6–7)
Job's outburst rouses the friends, and we hear the most venerable speak first. His kindly and persuasive tone cannot make his words less hurtful to Job; he proceeds complacently from a doctrine which, as we know from the Prologue, does not fit the facts. Job, who has no doubt often admonished those in trouble, must not give way to vexations now that he himself is troubled! What innocent person ever perished? But those who sow trouble surely reap it!

From these bland words, Eliphaz's position is becoming clear. Job must have sinned and will need to repent if he is to be saved. Yet Job was once highly respected, and it seems that Eliphaz has pondered on the matter. In the depth of night the answer has come to him. A spirit glided before his face, causing his bones to shake and his hair to stand on end. The eerie form addressed him, declaring that the semblance of human righteousness could not deceive God, before whom even the angels were accounted guilty. With this message to reinforce his views, Eliphaz has no difficulty in supposing that the apparently righteous Job has merited his misfortunes. He will find little support for a plea of righteousness from the angels who know themselves culpable in God's eyes. Such raging as Job's is the undoing of fools, hardened opponents of God, who suddenly lose children and property. Troubles like Job's are not without cause; and the cause is the faults which characterize humanity as certainly as sparks fly upward.

The best course for Job, then, is to seek God afresh and accept his guidance. Let him accept the corrective discipline of this suffering, returning to the right path from which (Eliphaz implies) Job has obviously strayed. Then the just God will make him happy again. The picture of bliss, as also the scheme of justice, is presented within the framework of this life. A reformed Job will find his property safe again, see many descendants, and come to his grave in ripe old age, as timely as corn brought to the threshing floor. Let Job hear this well-proven truth and act on it for his own good!

We feel the art of the dramatic poet in this typical speech from Job's friends—so eloquent, so right-sounding, that one could easily affirm it; and yet in fact so removed from truth and genuine sympathy.

Job's reply does not engage with the speech of Eliphaz in close argument. He clearly feels that his friend has not truly entered into his tragedy. If Job has indeed spoken wildly, are not his sufferings cause enough? The Almighty has shot arrows into him and his spirit drinks in their poison. In such a case, the conventional wisdom of Eliphaz, devoid of real sympathy, is like food without flavour; he declines it.

But oh that his prayer for death might be answered! He would be glad to die, all the more so because he has not disowned the commands of the Almighty (6.10). This thought is not developed here, but it will return more fully in later speeches.

How wounding is the attitude of the friends voiced by Eliphaz!

From such brothers (6.15) he looked for the kindness that endures through good times and bad. But they are like seasonal torrents when travellers find that the once gushing bed has dried up in summer's heat, the time of greatest need. Has he asked much of them, has he asked them to pay a ransom for him? They assume he has brought the calamity on himself; let them explain how he has erred and he will listen!

On the friends' view, the scale of Job's suffering would indicate a gross sin. Job reacts sharply against such implied calumnies from the best of his friends. It is as though they would grasp for a share in the property of the defenceless. He appeals to them to look upon him in truth, respecting justice:

> But now, please turn your eyes to me
> and in your faces I will tell no lie!
> Turn back, let no wrong be done,
> turn again, for my right is at stake!
> Is there wrong on my tongue,
> can my palate not discern evil? (6.28–30)

Unable to reach the understanding of his friends with such an appeal, Job now turns to God. His words in ch. 7 resemble the themes of the lamenting psalms, which reached out for God's compassion. A customary theme was the frailty of all human life. Here the view is even darker. To Job it seems that man's lifetime is like the hard toil of a servant's day, its end being looked for as blessed relief.

Job depicts before God his wretchedness in the manner of the psalmists: he portrays his sufferings in the long nights and fleeting days, and like the psalmists he calls on God to remember his transience. If help is to come, it must come soon, before he passes like a puff of air to the place of no return; God will look for him, but he will have gone (7.8b).

He calls to God without restraint. Why does he for ever harry him? The constant concern of God for man is a matter of thankful praise in the 'What is man?' of Psalm 8.4. But now this attention seems like a constant trial and torment:

> What is man that you should make much of him. . . ?
> How long will you not take your gaze from me
> nor leave me a moment to swallow my spittle? (7.17–19)

And if he has somehow slipped, why should this 'watcher of men'

make so much of it? Why will he not rather forgive? One day he will
come early to seek Job, and it will be too late. Thus with vehemence
and yet with childlike touch Job calls to God.

Bildad's first speech (ch. 8) and Job's reply (chs 9–10)

The second friend speaks, and we can have no great hopes of his sensitivity to Job. The anguished speech and lament have been to him
just a great wind, storm without substance, and he finds Job's stand
to be a slur on God's justice.

Does the Almighty pervert what is right? No doubt Job's children
have died because they sinned—the guarded expression of this
thought (8.4) may be due not so much to tact as to caution about
making false accusation. If Job will seek God's mercy and present
himself now as pure, God will certainly act to restore him. For God is
just, as generations of the fathers found; what can we, children of yes-
terday, know better than they? Their proverbs instruct us, and we
learn for example of the papyrus which grows so tall, but speedily collapses if its water dries up. So fall great men who forget God. The
case of Job is palpably behind Bildad's sumptuous imagery of the
prosperous man and his sudden downfall. But he assures him that if
he can now come before God as blameless, his joy will be restored.

To Bildad Job replies with ironic agreement. God will not reject a
just man—but how shall a man be just before God? Echoing Eliphaz
here (4.17ff.), he develops the words in a different sense: how should
a man *win the verdict* ('be declared right') before God? For his overwhelming power would prevent Job from stating his case. No less
than another, Job can hymn the Creator's power, which shakes the
earth, obscures the sun and stars, and in the beginning formed the
constellations and subdued the watery chaos (9.6–9). But where does
all this power leave the puny man seeking justice? Innocent, Job
would yet be confused into condemning himself; and we hear some of
his most extreme words, which he prefaces by saying he cares not to
safeguard his life:

> The devout and the wicked alike he destroys.
> If the scourge slays suddenly,
> he laughs at the trial of the innocent.
> Earth is given into the hand of the wicked,
> the eyes of her judges he blindfolds.
> If not he, then who? (9.22–24)

After thus contradicting Bildad's view of God's just government of the world, Job directs himself instead to God in lamenting style. He depicts his life as swiftly passing, swifter than a runner with tidings, swift as the papyrus boats on the Nile or as a great bird of prey. He fears that God will not clear him whatever he does. If he bathed himself white in snow, God would dash him into the mire before he could reclothe himself, so that the very clothes would abhor his approach. There can be no equality in contesting the case with God. There is no one superior to both who could enforce a ruling (9.33). Job longs to speak with him without the dread of his wrath.

Careless again of safeguarding his life, Job musters his strength to call to God with impassioned bitterness (10.1ff.): 'Show me the reason for your quarrel with me!' Is it good for God to abuse this poor creature of his, while beaming on the wicked? Do God's eyes make mistakes as men's do? Is he unjust like fallible men, assailing a person he knows to be innocent? And this is his own creature; God poured the semen into the womb like milk and curdled it like cheese, forming skin and flesh over a frame of intertwining bones and sinews. So Job came to life, a joyful existence in the faithful love of God, and preserved by God's constant care. And all the while, concealed in God's purpose were the calamities, whether Job sinned or whether he was righteous! It would have been better if they had carried him straight from the womb to the grave. If God would but look away and allow a short relief before Job goes for ever to the darkness and chaos of the land of the dead!

This cry to God, which ends rather like Psalm 39, gathers bitterness from the recollection of earlier days with him. God's work of creation, preservation and blessing appears in a fiendish light. It was all planned to lead up to this!

Zophar's first speech (ch. 11) and Job's reply (chs 12–14)
To Zophar's outraged ears, Job's reckless words have been like those of a scoffer. Job's assertion of his innocence has seemed like an impious contradicting of the all-knowing God, who no doubt could have found more fault with Job than he has done (11.6). This God of unfathomable wisdom unerringly picks out sinners for judgment and none can gainsay him. There are sinners too hardened to change (11.12), but Zophar still entertains a hope that Job will yet set his heart aright, put away his iniquity, and beseech God for forgiveness. Then his troubles will be like waters that have passed away.

Job in his turn is stung by Zophar's giving him a lesson on the greatness of God, along with his assumptions about Job's guilt. Job too knows that wise teaching which acknowledges the unfathomable wisdom of God. Such wise teaching will not die with the friends! Who does not know such things? Such mockery comes readily to the lips of those still at ease! 'The ruined man has got his deserts', they say, while all around robbers and braggarts fare well.

The customary wise teaching drew lessons from the animal world and ascribed understanding to the aged. Job takes up such words as though to outdo Zophar, and he excels him also in ascribing wisdom and power to God. But his account of God's acts (12.14–25) suggests the apparent arbitrariness of human destiny, especially in the ruin of respected leaders.

Vexed by his friends' application of traditional lore, Job hopes rather to argue his case with God (13.3). The friends are worthless healers. They just daub him with slander. Are they not afraid of the just God, that they would support God's case with falsehood? Let them listen as Job prepares to declare his innocence to God! They will be as witnesses at a sacred oath-ordeal—one could not swear a lie before the face of God and live; Job will stake his life on affirming his innocence before God (13.13–18; in 13.15 we may prefer the reading 'Though he may slay me, I will hope in him'). He is ready; where is his opponent? And then, when he has put his case, he will willingly die (13.19).

From here to the end of his speech, Job addresses the still hidden God. If only he would speak with Job plainly and without overwhelming terror, and show him where he has gone wrong! But he hides his face, treats him as an enemy, and leaves him to wonder what follies of youth may still count against him. And the suffering Job pictures himself as like a storm-driven leaf, a fettered prisoner, a moth-eaten garment.

Continuing in the lamenting style, Job lays before God the frailty and transience of mankind. Why judge such a poor creature so severely? Let him rather enjoy what he can from his few and troublous days! Soon he will go to the Underworld without hope of return.

Yet in this dark music we hear for a while a strain of tender yearning. Happy the trees which may sprout again after being cut to a stump! (some varieties were cut for this purpose):

For a tree there is still hope;
cut down, it may yet revive
and its shoots still rise.
Though its root has grown old in the ground
and its stump has died in the soil,
at the smell of water it will sprout
and form branches like a new plant.

But man dies and collapses,
he breathes his last, and where is he?
As waters drain from a lake
and a river wastes away and dries up,
so a man lies down and will not rise,
till the heavens are no more he will not waken
nor be roused from his sleep.

Oh that you would hide me in the Underworld,
that you would conceal me till your anger turned,
that you would set me a time to remember me!
If a man dies, will he live again?
All the days of my bondage I would hope
till my change came.
You would call and I would answer you,
for the creature of your hands you would yearn.
Then you would count my steps
without watching for my sin.
My offence would be sealed away in a bag,
and you would have buried my fault. (14.7–17)

But no! The reality is that the most valiant hope of man crumbles as a mountain-side gives way before torrents. God changes a man's bright face into the pallor of death. However his children fare, the dead man will know nothing of it.

Eliphaz's second speech (ch. 15) and Job's reply (chs 16–17)
Eliphaz cannot forget the beginning of Job's last speech, when he ironically disputed the friends' recourse to traditional wisdom. What kind of wise man is Job, speaking such hot air! Why, he is doing away with piety! His talk is evidence enough of his iniquity; no need for Eliphaz to show it! One would think he was the first man to be born, or that he has stood in God's inner council! But Eliphaz has the wisdom of years, for he is older than Job's father (15.10). Cannot Job

endure consoling counsel inspired by God and gently given, that he prates madly and huffs and puffs at God, blowing back at him the gift of breath? Let him remember that he is but man, of a race of sinners, and that even the angels and the heavens are not pure in God's eyes.

So Eliphaz comes to reiterate his doctrine, received from wise ancestors and untarnished by foreign notions (15.19). The wicked, he affirms, suffer continually. Even in prosperity they are ever in dread of sudden retribution. They suffer for their defiance of God, as when they brazenly settle in places God has cursed (15.28) or deal in bribes (15.34). Their wealth does not endure. Their just recompense will be paid in full and before its time. Eliphaz has the case of Job in mind, and his image of lost fruit on vine or olive alludes to Job's loss of children (15.33).

Indignantly Job retorts that his friends, with their unfeeling commonplaces, bring him grief rather than consolation. And so he passes to a lamenting description of the world of enmity which bears upon him, the attacks of God and of men (16.6–17). His diseased body is taken not as an object of pity but as proof of his guilt (16.8). The accusing attitude of the friends comes to seem like reviling, like physical attacks (16.10–11). But it is God's own assault which is felt most terribly:

> He grinds his teeth against me,
> like a foe he sharpens his eyes against me. . . .
>
> I lived peacefully, when he shattered me.
> Seizing me by the neck, he broke me.
> He set me up as his target,
> his archers surrounded me,
> he cleft my kidneys unsparingly,
> he poured my gall on the ground,
> he breached me with breach upon breach,
> he ran at me like a warrior. . . .
>
> On my eyelids falls the shadow of death,
> although no violence has stained my palms
> and my prayer is pure. (16.9, 12–17)

We feel the heroic quality of Job's struggle in face of this assault. Instead of despairing of all justice, Job cries:

> Earth, do not cover my blood
> and give no place for my cry to be laid to rest! (16.18)

He is anticipating his unjust death and asks that his remains, like those of a murdered man, should still cry out to heaven for justice. Furthermore he still holds the conviction that in heaven there is one that, unlike his friends, will support him as innocent, and tearfully he yearns for this upholder of truth and faithfulness to defend his case at the seat of power—and so Job finds he is quaintly praying for God to argue with God:

> Even now, look, my witness is in heaven,
> he who will testify for me is on high!
> While my earthly friends revile me,
> to God my eye is weeping
> that he would argue for a man with God
> as a man with his friend. (16.19–21)

The strange picture arises from the contradictions of experience: divine faithfulness and truth set against senseless devastation.

Job continues with the thought that he is almost lost to life:

> My few years being come,
> I must take the path of no return.
> My spirit is destroyed, my days extinguished.
> For me, the burial vault! (16.22–17.1)

Those about him offer only mockery and provocation. To the divine faithfulness alone he appeals, and again is led to a paradoxical conception as he calls to God:

> Give a pledge for me to yourself!
> Who else will go surety for me? (17.3)

Can God give the bail that will secure Job's release—can God give it to himself? But who else except God will in the end uphold truth and faithfulness, and at his own cost deliver the needy? A tremendous conflict rises in Job's vision, for in spite of the unchecked assault of evil, he will not let go his hold on the divine goodness. As for the mockers around him, God must not let them triumph! And a proverbial sentence (17.5) warns the friends of the penalties for false accusation.

The sequence in 17.6–10 is not obvious. Is Job thinking of the charge that he is doing away with piety (15.4)? His miserable condition, he says, is scandalous to the upright, but the righteous man holds on to his way and increases in strength—he does not take to

falsehood, like Job's friends. He challenges them to come on at him
again and prove once more their lack of wisdom.

Finally he reflects on the collapse of his purpose in life and of his
desires. He would gladly believe the night turning to day and, in the
darkness of his agony, sense the nearness of dawn. But what hope can
go with him into the Underworld, which is ready to close around
him?

> If I call the pit 'my father!',
> the worms 'my mother, my sister!',
> where then is my hope?
> My hope—who can see it?
> It will go down to the bars of the Underworld,
> we will descend together into the mire. (17.14–16)

Bildad's second speech (ch. 18) and Job's reply (ch. 19)

We find Bildad again showing little sympathy. How long will Job
keep up his tirades, tearing his own soul? Does he expect the estab-
lished order to be overturned for him? And Bildad simply reasserts
that the light of the wicked *is* put out; they receive just retribution.
His account of the calamities sent on the sinner again reflects Job's
plight, including his terrors, his diseased skin, his loss of children,
and the horror of all who hear of him.

Job feels the gross injustice and cruelty of this speech. If he has
erred, can they say how? (So 19.4, unless the thought is that his supposed error has not harmed them.) But the humiliation, from which
the friends make their slanderous deductions, has been unjustly
brought on him by God, he declares. It is God who has made him out
to be guilty, ignoring his cry of innocence. And Job laments his state
at length (19.7–20), depicting the sufferings God has heaped upon
him. From the highest honour he has been hurled down to the lowest
shame. His very household, brothers, wife, friends abhor him:

> Those that I loved have turned against me. (19.19)

His bones protrude through lacerated skin (19.20). Cannot his
friends, if nothing more, feel *pity*?

> Pity me, pity me, you, my friends,
> for the hand of God has struck me. (19.21)

Why must they persecute him as God does and never tire to slander
him (19.22)?

Oh that his plea of innocence could be indelibly inscribed! This wish (introducing a famous and much debated passage) implies a thought like that of 16.18–19. When he has perished, the appeal for vindication will remain, indestructible. That he anticipates his death may be indicated also by the contrast of v. 25: his redeemer (*gō'ēl*) will be *living*, and will act for him, standing hereafter on the earth. *Gō'ēl* is a legal term and denotes the one on whom the duty devolved to stand up for a person (usually his close relative), secure his rights or avenge his death. The thought here, then, is in part a warning to the slanderous friends, which is explicit in 19.28–29 (cf. 13.7–11; 17.5). There is one who will take his part, vindicate his innocence and punish those who have maligned him. And as the true 'witness' of 16.19f. eventually appears to be God himself, so here the 'redeemer' likewise seems to emerge in the person of God,

> whom I shall see on my side
> and my eyes shall behold, not estranged. (19.27)

So Job's conviction of divine truth and faithfulness again proves stronger than his experience of God as enemy.

At first the references to his flesh, eyes and sight (19.26–27) seem to complicate the picture. Is the vindication to come in time to save him from death? Or are his flesh and eyes to be restored in a resurrection after death? The context and comparisons with other passages suggest negative answers here. Rather, he is to die and enter the Underworld, land of no return, as described in other passages. But he will yet be granted the satisfaction of knowing that his innocence has been vindicated. 19.26b should then be rendered as RSV margin, 'without my flesh', while in 19.27 the 'eyes' and the 'seeing' will be poetical expressions of the satisfying knowledge granted to his shade. (That the dead could know either restlessness or peace is an idea evident in the great value put on proper burial.)

Thus the tremendous hold that Job maintains on his faith in God's goodness comes to expression once more. His horrible experiences all cry out 'God has wronged you! He is become your ruthless enemy!' But the conviction surges back: in the ultimate, in God, there is truth and fidelity. Though death finally takes Job's power to defend himself, God will appear for him, taking his part, clearing his name. At the wonderful prospect Job exclaims: 'My heart faints within me!' (19.27). How God would in practice vindicate him, and whether justice would really be satisfied by such an event, are questions not treated. All that the suffering Job holds to is his rock of faith, which now and then appears through the pounding waves: in the Ultimate is faithfulness and truth.

He concludes his speech by admonishing his friends: let them not continue to say that the root of his troubles is in his own errors (19.28), for false accusers should fear the sword of justice.

Zophar's second speech (ch. 20) and Job's reply (ch. 21)

Insulted by Job's view of the friends as slanderers, Zophar rushes into the fray. Job must realize that since man was first placed on earth there has been retribution for the wicked. Their joy is short-lived, for soon they are cut down and perish. Once again, the eloquent unfolding of this theme is meant to chime in with the fate of Job. The sinner, who may have crushed the poor or seized a property, is brought down from a great height, his children suffer, his food becomes poison to him, God's arrow pierces through his gall, his possessions are carried away. This is the fate of the wicked man, and so, he implies, we understand the fate of Job.

Job's reply, rather exceptionally, is a speech to his friend throughout, disputing the point he has made. He can defend himself against the slanderous imputation by pointing out how often the fates of men do not accord with their virtue. His experience has caused him to see the extent of such contradictions of justice and it makes him shudder with horror. He portrays wicked men who live long and prosperously, rich in children, secure houses, fertile cattle. Like a flock of lambs their children go forth dancing; there is music of song, framedrum, lyre and pipe. They die in peace, though caring nothing for God—a way of life Job hastens to forswear (21.16). How often does retribution, such as the friends have described, really fall? What do the wicked care if it is stored up for their descendants? True, one cannot teach God how to rule, but the fact is that death when it comes is the same for the fat man and for the starving, for one who has had every pleasure and for one who has had none.

Job knows too well the slanderous thoughts which govern their speeches (21.27–28). But let them enquire again about the fates of men. Many will be found to attest the prosperity of wicked men, who through their power escape even rebuke, and who are finally buried with great processions and vigils in a fine site, where even 'the clods of the valley-side are sweet for him'.

And how would you console me with such empty words?
Of all your answers there remains but treachery. (21.34)

Eliphaz's third speech (ch. 22) and Job's reply (chs 23–24)
The third round of exchanges is marked by open accusation against
Job. Eliphaz begins by declaring that since God is too great to be
enriched by men, he can have no motive for injustice. And he could
not be quarrelling with Job for his piety! Rather, Job must have
sinned. The sins must be so extensive that Eliphaz feels he can describe them by running through the categories relevant to a wealthy
man. Job must have exacted pledges of poor people accused of debt,
depriving them of their last garment. He must have failed to give
water or bread to the needy. He must have taken possession of land
by power rather than by right. He must have ill-treated the
undefended—widows and fatherless children. And now he is recom-
pensed! For God on high sees all, though the wicked imagine he does
not. Judgment falls on them, and their victims rejoice.

Finally, Eliphaz advises Job to agree with God and 'be at peace' by
repenting of his supposed sins. If he puts wickedness far from him
and returns to God in humble penitence, renounces greed for gold,
finding his treasure in God, then God will hear his prayer for healing
and soon Job will be fulfilling his vows of sacrifice with thanksgiving
for recovery (22.27).

This climax in the cruel accusation of the 'comforters' calls from
Job only renewed longing to put his case directly to God, so that the
cloud of false accusation be dispelled from him:

> Oh that I knew where I might find him
> that I might come to his seat of judgment...!
>
> Would he contend with me in overwhelming power?
> No, but he would take note of me.
> There an upright man could argue with him
> and I would be cleared for ever by my judge. (23.3–7)

Here again appears Job's ground-rock of faith, that in God he will
find truth. But the great waves soon dash over it. Where to find him?
Search as he may, Job cannot find the God who will heed his plea and
deliver him. But God knows where to find Job (23.10), and if he
would test him, Job would come out of it as proved gold. Against all
the calumnies of his friends he affirms:

> My foot has held to his step,
> his way I have kept and not swerved,
> from his lips' command I have not gone away,
> in my bosom I have stored the words of his mouth. (23.11–12)

But how can he struggle with God? God is sole sovereign and none can impede him from his purpose; he will accomplish what he has decreed for Job, and likewise for many others. This God is terrifying. He it is who appals Job, not the suffering itself (23.16–17, note RSV margin).

Unable himself to find the seat of the just Judge of the world to have his case rectified, Job reflects that his experience is only too typical. The world is full of injustices which go uncorrected by God (ch. 24). Why do the faithful not see him keeping times of judgment when he would save the afflicted? All kinds of wrong go unpunished. People shift landmarks, steal flocks and take the animals of widow and fatherless. The poor toil for the crops of the wicked, while they themselves are hungry and naked. As pledge for their debts, creditors seize even the babe from the breast.

> From out of the city the dying groan
> and the soul of the wounded cries for help
> and God does not heed the prayer. (24.12)

Under cover of darkness many wrongs go unpunished—murder, theft, adultery. The view that the perpetrators are swiftly snatched away like snow-waters in summer's heat (24.18–20) is presumably cited as that of the friends (and so RSV adds 'You say'). Job declares on the contrary that God prolongs the life of the oppressors and looks after them well. Death comes for them as it does for all (24.24 RSV margin). Who can deny it?

Bildad's third speech (ch. 25) and Job's reply (chs 26–27)
This short speech simply resumes the theme heard before (4.17; 15.14–16; and cf. Job in 9.2 and 14.4) that to the almighty God even the celestial bodies are not pure; how much less the maggot that is man!

This is the last utterance of the three friends, since the turn for a third speech does not come round to Zophar. We may wonder if words of Bildad and Zophar in this round have been lost or misplaced, especially since some of the lengthy material now ascribed to

Job (chs 26–31) seem to suit the friends' position rather than his. At this stage, however, let us continue to hear the speakers as the text presents them.

Job's reply makes ironical reference to the help and counsel offered by his friend (26.1–4). The passage which follows portrays the powerful acts of God in the universe, which men can hardly begin to understand. God's power is felt everywhere, and the Underworld (Sheol, Abaddon), hidden deep below the oceans, is naked to him. He spreads the canopy of the sky (or 'north') over chaos and hangs the earth over nothingness. He wraps waters in the clouds which hold without tearing. He covers the face of the moon, unfolding his cloud across it. He drew a boundary circle, the horizon, on the face of the waters, outside which is all darkness. Heaven's pillars tremble at his thunder-roar. At creation, by his power and skill the chaos-waters were tamed and divided (26.12); by his wind darkness was driven back and the chaos monster pierced (26.13). But all that we can know of his great works is but at the fringes. The grandeur we perceive is but a whisper of his power; who could contemplate its thunder?

In the mouth of Job this passage (26.5–14) shows that, in holding to his innocence, he is not unmindful of the power and mystery of God beyond human comprehension, and needs no instruction in it from the friends (cf. 9.5–13; 12.7f.); and it implies that the friends, with their confident explanations of God's dealings, are taking too much on themselves. If the passage was originally part of Bildad's speech, however, the point would be against Job, that he should not criticize ways of God that are beyond human comprehension.

In a fresh heading (27.1) we are told that Job again took up his poetic oration. The speech begins with his solemn and bitter oath by the life of the afflicting God, that so long as he has breath he will not speak falsely by accepting the friends' view; he will not misrepresent the integrity and rightness of his former life and accept the lie that he is suffering just retribution (27.2–6).

The speech continues by depicting the punishments which fall upon the wicked man. When trouble comes on him, God does not hear his prayer. His children are involved in his ruin. His gathering of wealth comes to nothing. He goes to bed rich and wakes up a pauper. The desert wind blows him from his place, an object of derision (27.7–23). This passage is difficult to align with the thoughts of Job. As the text stands, we may have to suppose that he is warning the friends against their falsehood, and does so ironically by echoing their

own doctrine of retribution. Such an intention is by no means
obvious. The passage sounds like a speech of the friends (with the exception of 27.11–12, addressed to a plural audience), and one must
wonder if the bulk of it is a survival from the missing third speech of
Zophar.

Job's poem on Wisdom (ch. 28)

Still under the heading of Job's poetical oration (27.1), a well-knit
poem is unfolded. Its theme is that man is able to search out remote
and hidden things like precious metals and stones, but he cannot find
and possess the divine wisdom.

For silver there is a mine, for gold a place where men refine it.
From earth and stone are extracted iron and copper, and shafts are
driven deep into the darkness; in remote valleys miners hang and
sway far beneath the foot of the traveller. The earth which gives food
above is overturned below as the miners quarry and search (some
think the 'fire', 28.5, was used to split rocks in a process of heating
and dousing); here is the place of lapis lazuli, with its glittering par-
ticles (28.6), along paths the keen-eyed falcon cannot glimpse nor the
regal lion tread. Flint rock and mountains give way before the miner,
as he cleaves channels to reach every precious stone. River-sources he
searches and he brings to light hidden treasure.

All this can men track down and take in their hands. But where is
the place of 'wisdom', the divine skill of God's hands in creation?
This Wisdom man cannot know, nor can the deeps of the world tell
her secret. The great wealth of gold, silver, jewels, coral, crystal or
pearls cannot purchase her. She is hidden from all living creatures
and the realms of the dead have heard but a report of her.

God alone knows where she is. At the beginning of all things, when
he made the wind with its fine weight and apportioned the waters
with a measure, when he made the law of the rain and a path for the
storm, then God looked upon Wisdom, summed her up, understood
her and searched her deeply. The figure of Wisdom thus represents
the mystery and order of creation, an ultimate depth of beauty and
truth in creation which is known only to God.

At the end of the poem we find a verse of different rhythm, using
the divine name Adonay ('Lord'; the only occurrence in Job, and
found elsewhere in the mouth of God only four times in a formula in
Ezekiel); the verse defines wisdom for man as the fear of the Lord and
the avoiding of evil. There is some question, then, whether this verse

was part of the original poem. As it stands it rounds off the poem positively. Man, though unable to grasp the divine Wisdom, receives a word from God to set him on a wise path: live in awe of God's reality, shun wickedness!

Clear in itself, the poem of ch. 28 is difficult to relate to the struggle of Job. His wrestling with the accusations of his friends and the silence of God has yet to reach its climax in his final statement of innocence and appeal (chs 29–31) and has yet to be resolved in the appearing of God who himself will show, and with irony, the unattainable marvels of his wisdom (chs 38–42). The possibility that ch. 28 has been added to the original work may be borne in mind. As it stands, it makes a calm interlude in Job's turbulent journey.

Job's final plea (chs 29–31)

A fresh rubric, worded as 27.1, states that Job again took up his poetical speech. The friends are not directly addressed or referred to. There is a short direct address to God in 30.20–23, as Job works his way from lamenting reflections to a final appeal for his case to be heard (31.35f.).

The first theme (ch. 29) is the recollection of former days; the recounting of their happiness will make the following lament (ch. 30) the more piteous by contrast. On that former life God's light shone and his protection was strong:

> Oh that I were as in the months of old,
> as in the days when God guarded me,
> when he shone his lamp over my head
> and by his light I walked through the darkness! (29.2–3)

Those were his 'autumn' days, when his life had yielded much fruit, thanks to the Almighty's protection and favour. His children were about him, and great was the yield of his animals and fields (29.6). The community held him in highest esteem. When he took his seat in the town's gateway, the place of deliberation and judgment, the young fell back out of sight, the old rose and remained standing, princes checked their words and chiefs in awe fell silent. All spoke well of him because he came to the rescue of the defenceless. The needy blessed him for giving them joy. So 'righteousness' and 'justice' were his clothing—the righteousness which stands up for the oppressed. He was eyes to the blind man and feet to the lame. He was 'father' to the poor, defending and providing. He would look deeply into the grievances of strangers. He broke the fangs of the wicked to make them drop their prey. He expected then to live to a great age in honour and happiness.

And his place in the community again fills his thoughts. All were silent when he spoke, and after he had spoken. Eagerly they drank his words, which came like sweet rain on the thirsty. He cheered them when they lost faith; they could not dim the light from his face. They looked to him for decisions, as to a chief or king. Confident in times of alarm, he was like a consoler in the midst of mourners.

From this pinnacle of respect Job has been hurled to utter degradation. In his tightly knit community this was no doubt the greatest suffering he had to bear. He is mocked by the very outcasts of the people, and mere youths at that. He depicts these wretches who barely subsist around the margins of the society (30.1–8). He could not have employed their fathers with his sheep-dogs, so feeble they were. These are people who live from wild plants and roots, chased from society like thieves, huddling in caves and scrub. And now, finding one who from his wealth always fed the hungry, they only jeer at his downfall. He describes their terrifying harassment (30.9–15). The contrast with his former respect could not be greater. His princely honour is chased away as a cloud before the wind.

For the last time Job gathers up his anguish in lament before God (30.16–31). In such lament the soul itself is poured out, as the whole experience of the suffering grips the mind of the sufferer (30.16). He tells of the pain that bores and gnaws, and binds his throat like a collar. That the lament is an appeal to God becomes clear:

> I have cried to you for help but you do not answer,
> I stand praying and you just observe me.
> You have changed and become cruel to me,
> with the force of your hand you persecute me.
> You make me ride on the wind
> and fling me about in the tempest.
> I know you will return me to death,
> appointed home for all the living,
> but from a ruin does one not stretch out a hand,
> from disaster cry for rescue?   (30.20–24)

Job pleads that he wept for the afflicted. Expecting good from God, he himself has received disaster. His intestines boil, his skin has turned black. No one can bring him solace; he cries in vain for help 'in the assembly', that is, perhaps, in the gathering of his comforters. He is brother rather to the jackals and ostriches, whose eerie cries ring in desert places. The music of his life has turned to wailing.

Job now swears his innocence of such sins as might be supposed to have brought on him his troubles. The first sin that he denies (31.1) is lust against a virgin: he laid an obligation ('covenant') on his eyes not to lead him to such sin, which he knew could not escape God's all-seeing eye.

His declaration then passes into the form of the conditional self-curse: 'If I have done thus and thus, let such and such befall me!' In this way he repudiates sins of fraud and corruption which are not precisely defined (31.5–8). Next he denies the sin of the adulterer, enticed by a married woman and hiding near his neighbour's door to observe when he goes out; the curse that he invokes would strike him through his own wife (a conception of solidarity strange to us), she being snatched away to slavery and rape.

He has not refused redress to his servants when they made complaint. He knew too well that God himself would make enquiry on their behalf:

> Did not he who made me in the womb
> make him also?
> Did not the same one
> fashion us both in the womb? (31.15)

If he has turned away the widow, or eaten alone without sharing his portion, in family fashion, with the fatherless; if he has passed by the cold and naked or used his power in court against the fatherless, then let the arm that failed to help or rose to bully be broken from its socket! Behind the undefended, he always remembered, was the majesty of the unseen divine defender.

He denies making gold his god (31.24–25), congratulating himself on his wealth. Nor has he thrown a kiss of homage to the rising sun or the moon gliding in beauty. He has not rejoiced at an enemy's ruin, or attacked him with a curse. He has not begrudged hospitality; those eating with him have found food enough and to spare (31.31). He has not refused lodging to wayfarers. He has not lived a secret life of sin.

Breaking into this last denial, Job expresses impulsively the aim of his long speech of lament and protestation. He is striving for a hearing from God the judge and righter of wrongs:

> Oh that I had one to hear me!
> Behold, my signature!
> Let the Almighty answer me! (31.35)

He has put his mark attesting his plea of innocence. Oh that he had the
document of his opponent's accusations, after so long being kept in
ignorance! He would carry it proudly on his back or bind it as a royal
turban round his head. He would give a full account of all his deeds,
presenting it unashamed like a prince.

From this irruption, he returns to the orderly progress of his oaths
of clearance (31.38–40; some prefer to explain the position of this
passage as an error): if the soil that he tilled wept and cried out against
him, for having expropriated and done away with the original
owners, let him reap thorns and stinking weeds! So ends the last oration of Job. All that he could say in appeal for a fair hearing he has
said, and a note records, 'The words of Job are completed'.

The Intervention of Elihu (chs 32–37)

Introduction to Elihu (32.1–6a)
A short prose narrative now introduces another speaker. His name is
Elihu and his ancestry is noted (which was not the case for Job and his
friends). Being younger than the others, he has hitherto held back.
But he is now moved to speak by his anger at Job's claim to be right
over against God and at the petering out of the friends' rebukes. Even
in these few verses we may notice that the style is inferior to that of
the Prologue, being laboured and repetitious.

Elihu's first speech (32.6–33.33)
Elihu's poetic oration now begins and is to continue for six chapters.
Occasionally there are fresh headings (34.1; 35.1; 36.1), dividing the
address into four parts; but there is no reply from any other speaker
nor any reference to Elihu in any other part of the book.

He begins by explaining why he must command the attention of his
elders. It is not age itself, but God's spirit in a man, which gives
insight, and such an inspiration Elihu evidently believes he has.
Indeed, from such abundance of the spirit within him, he is bursting
to speak. He remarks on the failure of the friends to vanquish Job,
and he promises to speak without fear or favour.

He then turns to Job (33.1ff.) and again builds up expectation of the forthright, challenging discourse still to come. Rather pompously, we may feel, he seems to be offering himself in the place of God. If Job fears the inequality of arguing with God, let him answer Elihu, who, being a fellow mortal, need not terrify him.

Coming at last to his argument (33.8ff.), Elihu first summarizes what he takes to be Job's claim: he is without sin, yet God attacks him as an enemy. Elihu has not in fact understood the position of Job, who does not claim to be sinless, but to be innocent of such offences as could explain his peculiar fate.

For Elihu, the greatness of God over man nullifies all criticism (33.12). Of course God has answered Job! The very fears he sends in the night are like words of warning. Sickness is a chastening to turn a man back from his wicked course. The way of repentance is offered to him, it may be through one of the multitude of angels (a 'mediator' or 'interpreter', 33.23). So God grants him deliverance from death (33.24; it is not clear whether the angel, successful in securing repentance, has provided the ransom-payment that substitutes for the death). The health of such a penitent is then restored and he can attend the sanctuary and give thanks, testifying in a psalm that though he sinned, God forgave him and spared his life. If a man will not heed the warning, God will try again, twice, thrice! But in the case of the unrepentant Job, Elihu implies, God's warnings fall on deaf ears.

Elihu's second speech (ch. 34)
Elihu now commands attention from 'wise men' rather generally and invites them to consider the issue. Again he gives his summary of Job's stand and at once characterizes it as that of an arch-scoffer; Job has united himself with the wicked, for he has denied the justice of God.

This justice Elihu then affirms (34.10ff.) arguing from the nature of God as sole ruler of all, on whose breath all life depends. Consideration of God's power is enough basis for Elihu. The actual happenings in the world and in the case of Job he quite ignores. So we hear his account of a world where corrupt tyrants and wealthy men are speedily struck down by divine judgment. It is not for such to go to court with God. He needs no enquiry to establish guilt, but brings down the wicked in an instant. But the manner and timing of his judgments are his alone to decide (34.29).

And if someone repents, is God to refuse forgiveness because Job

disallows the way of repentance? This poorly expressed passage
(34.31–33) is perhaps ironical, as though Job presumed to do God's
work for him. Men of right thinking, Elihu is sure, will share his in-
dignation at Job's harangues against God and wish him 'to be tried to
the end'.

Elihu's third speech (ch. 35)

Elihu recommences with an address to Job. He will answer him and
his friends at the same time (35.4). God, he argues, is so great and
lofty that he has nothing to gain or lose from men's actions, and so he
has no reason to be unjust (cf. Eliphaz 22.2f., Job 7.20). When
oppressed people cry out and are not saved, it is because they have
not truly prayed to God as their maker, acknowledging that he 'gives
songs in the night'—cause for thanksgiving in the darkest hour. How
much less will he deliver when Job rails against him!

Elihu's fourth speech (chs 36–37)

With another grand introduction Elihu calls on Job to await further
instruction; 'one complete in knowledge is before you'. He takes up
again his theme of affliction as corrective discipline. Those who heed
the warning and repent of their sins are delivered to complete their
full number of days in contentment. Those who reject the warning
perish by violence.

Job might by now have been brought from distress to a situation of
ease, but he has cherished anger rather than repentance. Is he joining
the scoffers and takers of bribes (RSV 'ransom' 36.18)? From such
people the loudest cries will not be answered.

And who can say to the mighty God, 'You are wrong'? Rather, one
should praise God in the manner of the hymns (36.24ff.). He is
beyond our knowing. The wonders of rain, clouds, thunder and
lightning are his doing.

Elihu continues in this vein at length (37.1ff.). His heart leaps at
the crash of thunder and he recognizes the great things of God beyond
human understanding. He speaks of snow and wild beasts, whirl-
wind, ice, rain and lightning, the balancing of the clouds, the hot still-
ness before the desert wind, the canopy of the skies. Does Job
understand these wonders? Can he do God's work? Against such a
God does one take up a case? One might as well ask to be swallowed
up! We cannot bear to gaze at a bright sky, let alone at God! Radiance
from the northern sky (the Northern Lights or shining rain?) sug-

gests the golden robe of God, but him we cannot see. Justice is his, and men should turn to him in worship rather than in pride of wisdom.

Elihu's exposition of God's mighty works and the appropriate human attitude is perhaps the most impressive part of his speeches. Even here, however, there continues to be a clumsiness of expression and order, which produces several obscurities in the Hebrew (e.g. 36.16–21, 23; 37.12–13, 17).

The Lord Speaks with Job (38.1–42.6)

God's first speech (38.1–40.2) and Job's response (40.3–5)

All Job's passionate striving has been towards 'finding' God: a meeting where he could discover what has turned God against him and where he could defend himself against unjust charges; a meeting where each could speak directly and the impenetrable darkness over his fate would be dispelled. He has waited long, and human counsellors, for whom doctrine was stronger than love, have added greatly to his ordeal.

But now the longed-for event takes place, introduced not by a narrative but a brief rubric: 'And the Lord answered Job from a storm'— the fiery tempest traditionally linked with his manifestations. He speaks:

> Who is this who darkens counsel
> by words without knowledge? (38.2)

It is as though Job had just ended his final appeal and the long oration of Elihu had never been delivered. It is to Job alone that God speaks. Already a rebuke is implied. Job's words about God's dealings with the world are without knowledge and only obscure the purposes of God. With irony he is summoned to gird up his loins like a combatant before the fray and inform God on the questions which are now to be put. With irony, too, he is asked if he can do the Creator's work or comprehend its wonders.

The marvels are surveyed in superb poetry. Its splendid flow contrasts with the laboured style of Elihu, and there is no tirade against Job. The point that Job has not the knowledge to sit in judgment on God is indeed tellingly brought home, but no charges are made. In the long speeches of God we shall hear no discussion of the questions which have animated Job and his friends—Job's guilt or innocence, the reason for his calamities, the justice of God's dealings with men.

Question after question comes to Job. Questions are the most arresting form of address and here bring home to the full the weight of the theme: the surpassing wonder and beauty of the Creator's work. And these great questions come to Job from the mouth of the Creator himself, God manifest before him. Was Job present at the foundation of the earth, which, like the foundation of a building, was celebrated with songs of joy? What information can he give about the birth of the sea, when it burst from the womb and God confined it and swaddled it in clouds, and set its limits with cliffs and shores?

Thus with the flow of questions come the brilliant poetic flashes, strokes of a master painter that convey the wonder of each element. As the angel of dawn darts across the skies, removing the darkness, she seems to take up the fringes of earth's night coverlet and shake out the nocturnal marauders. As daylight grows from the east, lines and forms of relief appear in distant landscapes, as on clay impressed with a seal.

And what of the unsearchable distances (38.16ff.), the depths where the land of the dead is hidden, the ends of the earth, and the home from which God daily leads out to work the light and darkness? What of the snow-stores above the skies, and the stocks of hail kept ready like sling-stones? What of the ways made for the lightning and the violent desert wind, the thunderbolts and rainstorms? Where no man lives, the storm still comes and soaks the wastes and they grow green. Who fathered the rain and the dewdrops? Who bore the ice and the hoar frost?

More wonders of God's work in the heavens are presented (38.31ff.). Can Job bind up the stars in their clusters or lead them on their course? Can he, like God, dispose the heavenly bodies which in turn regulate events on earth (38.33)? Can Job take God's place when he commands lightnings as ready servants, takes stock of the clouds, or tilts the waterskins of the skies?

Wonder is stirred next at the life of animals (38.39ff.), especially the wild creatures whose wisdom owes nothing to man. God alone is their helper and guide. Lion and raven look to him for food. He counts the months when the ibex or the hind is with young, and he is ready to be their midwife. None but he has given the wild ass freedom in the rocky wilderness, where he can laugh at the tumult of the towns and the shouts of the drivers. Disdainful of man's service also is the wild ox, much as man would like to use his great strength.

The strange behaviour of the ostrich got her the reputation of being stupid and careless of her eggs, but if God has not made her seem wise, he has given her a glory of speed. Assisted by furious flapping, her immense strides let her mock the fastest riders. (The passage, 39.13–18, deviates from the form of the pressing questions and was not represented in the Greek translation.)

The questions are resumed. Who but God can give strength and courage to the war-horse? As the cavalry prepares for battle, he paws the ground and shakes his mane and snorts in his eagerness. At the signals of the horn he neighs and gallops as if he would swallow the ground. And is it by Job's wisdom that the hawk soars and migrates to the south? By God's instruction alone the eagle can nest on a pinnacle of rock and see his prey from an immense height.

The Lord now invites Job to reply (40.1–2). Let the critic of God begin his argument! But Job will only say that he is unworthy; he has spoken too much already and will speak no more.

We recall that in earlier speeches Job has anticipated that he would not be able to argue his case with God. Who could oppose the mighty Creator and say 'What are you doing?' (9.1–12). Lost in an unequal contest, he would be confused into condemning himself (9.14–20). In the event, the divine revelation and words are indeed conveying to Job the awesomeness of God, but the question of guilt or innocence has not been raised, and Job's mind, far from being bludgeoned and confused, has been led to a fine contemplation of natural wonders. Pictures of oceans and skies, dawning, storms and stars have been followed by vignettes of animal life: the birth of a little creature in the wilderness, the free running of the wild ass, the eager spirit of a horse, the eagle's eye. Great and small speak of wonder and love. Job senses the divine and feels unworthy. He is not crushed by sheer power. He is taken up with the beauty and mystery and has no appetite for re-asserting his case.

God's second speech (40.6–41.34) and Job's response (42.1–6)
The Lord begins a second speech, headed as before. Again he proposes questions for Job to answer. Must Job accuse God in order to clear himself? Can he undertake the mighty tasks of God? Let him, the critic, put on the mantle of God and mete out universal justice, and God himself will praise him!

Thus the message of God's first speech is presented a second time,

as it were for its better confirmation. Job's denunciations of the
divine government are again treated with irony. But as before, the
speech soon passes to contemplation of wonders, and even the
questioning now is little in evidence.

> Behold, the Beast which I made along with you!
> He eats green stuff like cattle! (40.15)

And a most remarkable animal, Hebrew 'Behemoth', is then pictured
in detail (40.15–24). It may be the hippopotamus, or a kind of mythical prototype, a super-hippopotamus which would still be a reality to
the ancient imagination. We wonder at his mighty muscles and
limbs, and hear of his creation at the beginning of all things (40.19a);
only his creator is his master (40.19b). He has his own happiness.
Peaceably the hills give him of their crops and the wild creatures
'rejoice' there—as though feasting and dancing with him. How he
enjoys the shade of lotus trees, the cool reeds of the marshland, or the
poplars of the torrent-bed! With the strength God has given him, he
need not fear the river-flood or the attacks of hunters.

One more animal picture is presented, filling the rest of God's
poetical speech. The questions are resumed for a while. Can Job, like
God, deal with this tremendous creature?

> Can you draw Leviathan with a hook
> or fasten his tongue with a cord? (41.1)

This time the picture resembles the crocodile, but mythical features
are more marked (41.18–21) and the name 'Leviathan' indicates the
primeval monster which God mastered at creation ('Ltn' in the
tablets from Ugarit). The subdued monster was thought of as still
surviving, sometimes glimpsed at play in the great waters
(Ps.104.26). Can Job, like God, tame and play with him?

God speaks like an enthusiastic poet:

> I will not keep silence over his limbs,
> nor over his strength and the grace of his build! (41.12)

Leviathan is armour-plated with rows of shields, joined so that nothing can penetrate. With his sneezing come flashes of light, and his
eyes glow red like the dawn; he breathes out smoke and flame (some
relate all this to steam and sunlit spray from the surfacing snout of the
crocodile). Like attendants, 'glory' lodges on his neck, while 'con-
sternation' dances ahead of him. The folds of his flesh are cast hard;

his heart too is cast hard as a lower millstone. When he stirs, heroes panic and hide. The strongest weapons are as straw to him. His under-scales cut into the mire like teeth of a threshing-sled. He lashes the deep till it froths like an ointment-pan and he leaves behind him a foaming wake. There is not the like of him on earth; he is king over all proud beasts.

Here the catalogue of wonder ends without more ado. God who alone could make and sustain these marvellous beings has depicted them with enthusiasm. He adds no words of moralizing or reproof. With his last picture of marvel he is done.

Job's response is again short (42.1ff.). He acknowledges that God can accomplish all. The questions of God still echo in his mind— 'Who is this who obscures God's purposes. . . .?'—and he confesses he has spoken ignorantly of things too wonderful for him. God has invited him to inform him on the marvels of creation. But he has only desire to speak of his new experience:

> I had heard of you only by hearsay,
> but now my own eyes have seen you.
> Therefore I melt away, sorrowing
> on the dust and ashes. (42.5–6)

(The translation 'melt away' seems possible here, as also in 7.5,16; if the more common meaning 'reject, despise' is preferred, the object understood will be 'myself' or, less likely, the statements referred to in 42.3. The word rendered 'sorrowing' often does not refer to repentance from sin, so 'repenting' could be misleading here; with the previous verb it seems to form a hendiadys, both words combining to depict Job's self-abasement in the direct experience of God.)

These words are the resolution of the long struggle. Job does not repent in the sense that the friends had counselled, confessing to sins as the cause of his sufferings. But the immediacy of his encounter with God has filled him with such a sense of God that he can only express his unworthiness. The most amazing thing is that the man who, by God's own testimony, had lived as the best of God's servants, has now found such a new depth of knowledge of God that his former knowledge seems but that of hearsay. By a path of terrible loss and anguished spiritual struggle, and while still in the dark valley, he has reached his new vision, far surpassing the religion of his prosperity.

The Epilogue (42.7–17)

The conclusion of the story is told in prose. No reference is made to the heavenly council and the reason for Job's ordeal. But the narrator makes sure that the friends and their sympathizers do not congratulate themselves on having been proved right. Any satisfaction they have been feeling at the abasement of Job is quickly dispelled. The Lord speaks to their leader, Eliphaz: 'My anger is kindled against you and your two friends, for you have not spoken concerning me truth as my servant Job has'. He further commands them to offer up burnt offerings of seven bulls and seven rams and to have Job pray for them to be forgiven. Only by Job's prayers will God be restrained from breaking out upon the friends. The verdict of God could hardly be more decisive. As for Elihu, who made so much of his intervention, he is ignored.

The friends do as they are bidden, and Job's prayer avails for them. His generous and forgiving prayer for his friends was answered, and the Lord now restored Job in health and happiness with double measure. Family and community gathered about him in happy consolation and celebration. The doubled blessing of God was shown in his doubled herds. More children were born—seven or perhaps fourteen sons (the Hebrew number has an unusual form). Too many daughters, in view of the troubles of marriage settlements, might not be thought a good thing; the number stayed at three—but three of the dearest and most beautiful there had ever been. A whole new life-span, and twice over, was granted to Job, and he rejoiced to see his great-great-grandchildren before he died, an old man full of days.

2

GATHERING OUR
OBSERVATIONS:
STRUCTURE AND THEME

N OW THAT WE HAVE LISTENED carefully to the narrator and the
dramatic speakers in the Book of Job and become familiar with
all its parts, we can gather and develop our impressions. We have
noticed some problems in the relationship of the parts and that the
book may not always have been in the form that we have received.
Let us therefore survey its structure with the question of growth in
mind. We shall then be able to gather our impressions of 'theme',
considering the leading ideas in the parts and in the whole.

1. The basis in a folk tale

We found the most obvious structural feature in the book to be the
distinction between the prose narrative and the poetic speeches. The
Prologue and Epilogue remind us of folk-stories, with repetition of
wording, symmetry of events, the uncomplicated perfection of Job,
and attention to details such as the numbers of the herds and the children. God, who is generally referred to here as 'Yahweh', the Lord, is
portrayed with a certain crudity—provoked by the Satan (2.3), liable
to deal 'rashly' (so the Hebrew of 42.8) with the offending friends.
The narrative is memorable and enthralling.

The poetic speeches begin in startling contrast as Job utters his
curse. The atmosphere of propriety is rent as the speakers exchange
abuse and threats and Job pours out his soul in defiance and piteous
lamentation. In the poetry the name 'Yahweh' is generally absent,
and the majesty and mystery of God are portrayed in elevated style.
The poetic section does not hark back obviously to details of the
story; the speeches of God in particular are surprisingly aloof from
any reference to the nature and circumstances of Job's ordeal. Again,
the Epilogue may surprise us with its simple and absolute verdict for

Job and against the friends, in view of the ironically critical tone of God's previous speeches to Job.

Can we explain such differences by supposing that the prose story of Job was already in existence before the great poet decided to take it as a convenient framework? It is interesting that Ezekiel, who refers to Noah, Daniel and Job as outstandingly righteous men (Ezek. 14.12–20), probably reflects here popular traditions about ancient patriarchs. Like the patriarchal stories of the Pentateuch, the prose story reflects an ancient way of life, with natural charm. We notice the wealth counted in flocks, herds and servants, the piety of the head of the family who offers sacrifices, the interest in hospitality, gifts and wonderful length of life. The 'silver piece' of Job 42.11 is mentioned elsewhere only with reference to Jacob (Gen. 33.19; Jos. 24.32). We can hardly think of deliberate imitation of the patriarchal stories here, as the substance of our story is quite different. But we may well assume a similar milieu of traditional story-telling. Altogether, it seems likely that there was an ancient story of Job and that the use of it accounts for some of the contrasts we have noted.

Even so, there are grounds for maintaining that the poet has retold the story for his own purpose. We note the extremely fine style evident in the Prologue, an excellence worthy of the great poet, if not unique to him in Hebrew literature. We note the suitability of the Prologue in creating just the situation the poet needs for his speeches, establishing all along the innocence of Job and the error of the plausible friends. And we note that the Prologue and the Epilogue do not together constitute a complete story. To what would the final verdict of the Lord refer? A middle would be missing, and if we try to imagine what it could have been—for example, friends joining wife in advising Job to curse God—we are reduced to speculation.

> A bold attack on the incongruities has recently been made by V. Maag in his *Hiob* (1982). He distinguishes two sources: (1) an independent novel about an Aramean Job (1.1–2.10 and 42.11–17), and (2) an account of an Edomite Job that framed the main poetic dialogue (2.11–13 and 42.7–9). When a later compiler joined these two works, Maag has to assume, much material from both stories was lost. Speculation is thus again obliged to be elaborate!

We may do better, then, to look for fundamental unity between the prose story and the poetic dialogue. We can recognize that the poet used and skilfully retold the old story to serve his purpose, using even the difficulties to good effect. We can explain that the heavenly scenes of the Prologue are not referred to again because they have served their purpose, and because men on earth do not receive such explanations of their fates. And the verdict is given so decisively for Job against the friends because the poet, though showing God as awesome and sovereign before Job, still wishes there to be no shadow of doubt on the fundamental issue. As for the contrast between the patient and the passionate Job, the poet may have been glad of it as dramatically very effective.

2. Problems in the third cycle of speeches

Job's three friends all speak and are answered in turn. Twice the turn goes round in due order. Then Eliphaz begins the third cycle and is duly answered. Bildad takes his turn but is exceptionally brief (ch. 25), while Zophar misses his turn altogether. Job's reply to Bildad is long (he holds the stage from chs 26–31), has an unnecessary heading in 27.1 (cf. 26.1; 29.1), and contains passages that sound like arguments of the friends (26.5–14; 27.7–10, 13–23) and a poem that seems to lie outside the debate altogether (ch. 28).

Taken together, these facts indicate that the third cycle has undergone change in transmission. It is tempting to reconstruct speeches for Bildad and Zophar out of the passages that sound inappropriate on the lips of Job. But one can only speculate on various ways of doing this and one cannot know whether some material has been dropped altogether. Effort may be better spent in trying to read the present text as positively as possible. The petering out of the friends' speeches has a certain suitability in view of their inadequacies. And when Job, in the present text, describes the greatness of God (26.5–14), we can accept that his position in fact never denied this, and we shall be all the more ready to evaluate God's manifestation in chs 38–42 in terms of direct experience rather than instruction.

More difficult is the passage where Job describes at length the punishments of the wicked (27.7–23). Encouraged by the verses clearly addressed to the plural (27.11–12), we must attempt to see this as an ironical warning to the falsely accusing friends, turning their own words against them; we might just imagine one of our great actors conveying this sense by tone and gesture. We can hardly take this passage as evidence that Job has come to a more orthodox frame of mind, as this would weaken the dramatic development of the whole work, with its turning point in the manifestation of God and Job's response.

One may wonder if the preservation of the third cycle was affected by the difficulty the devout transmitters continued to feel in what seemed to be outrageous utterances by Job. Prompted by God's siding with Job in the Epilogue, did the traditionists incline to furnish Job with more orthodox utterances at the end of his debate, at the expense of the condemned friends? The possibility reminds us what a disturbing work this was, and what a marvel it is that it has reached us, in the main, unblunted.

The beautiful poem on Wisdom (ch. 28) is another matter. Placed now as a continuation of Job's speech, it does not seem to belong to the controversy between the speakers, to whichever side we allocate it. Instead of the style of spirited argument, we have a meditative poem with a refrain (vv. 12 and 20). The three names for God most characteristic of the rest of the speeches are not chosen here (vv. 23 and 28). Moreover, the outlook here attributed to Job would forestall the speeches of God in chs 38–39 (28.26b and 38.25b are identical in the Hebrew). The signs are, then, that ch. 28 was not part of the original work. However, since the theme of the unsearchableness of the divine wisdom harmonizes well with the speeches of the Lord (chs 38–41), and since the poetry is of excellent quality, we can well attribute it to the author of the book or his circle, where a fine poetic tradition surely flourished. We may then imagine that, in the circles where *Job* was recited, the love of poetry sometimes prevailed over the sense of drama, and so this fine meditation, independently composed, came to be included at this point for its own merits. Like some musical cadenzas, it enhances the progress of the work only by offering a reflective pause. The audience rests for a while from the great tensions, charmed and refreshed by the skilful variations on the theme.

3. The episode of Elihu

Job's appeal for God to answer rises to its final climax, and God responds from the tempest, 'Who is this who darkens counsel?' But between appeal and answer lies the long episode of Elihu (chs 32–37). The words of God should refer to the previous speaker, but because of Elihu's intervention we must now take them to refer to the previous speaker but one! Thus we are already inclined to regard the

Elihu episode as a later insertion into the work. Several further considerations bear this out.

The style of the Elihu poetry and introductory prose is markedly inferior to that of the rest of the book: it is prolix, clumsy and often obscure. Unlike the other characters, Elihu is furnished with a genealogy. There is no hint of Elihu in any other part of the book, not even in the Lord's comments on the speakers in the Epilogue. Unlike all the other speakers, he delivers a succession of four orations without receiving any response. He seems to be at some distance from the drama as he summarizes and cites Job's speeches and undertakes a comprehensive rebuttal (33.9–11; 34.5–6; 35.2–3). In the more impressive part of his oration he seems to be influenced by the following speeches of the Lord (especially 37.14–18). As in style, so also in thought the Elihu episode is inferior, inasmuch as it grandiosely purports to correct the previous speakers, while it actually misunderstands Job and offers inappropriate arguments which have already been better expressed by the friends.

The pomposity of Elihu is so conspicuous and at times laughable (32.17–22; 36.2–4) that one could almost think the author intended a caricature. One could imagine the original poet's work arousing the ire of some authorities and his obliging them by adding Elihu as their mouthpiece, skilfully winning their approval, but making his scorn of them clear to the discerning. However, the difference of style rules this out, and it is not likely that a later, poorer poet would effect this subtlety. Rather, some later poet will have added this section, indignantly determined to state the correct view and counter the shocking words of Job, and yet failing to comprehend the original poet's thought. Unwittingly the later poet has revealed his arrogance and lack of discernment, and left himself exposed to implicit condemnation in the Epilogue. For if Job is pronounced right, Elihu, no less than the friends, must be wrong.

In the end, the paradoxical effect of the Elihu episode is to deal another blow at the opposition to Job. The doctrinaire opposition has been given one more opportunity, and an extended one, to show itself for what it is, even coming between the sufferer and God. So the eventual triumph of Job and the rout of his critics are all the more emphatic. True, Elihu has passages, as the friends have also, which are convincing in themselves, as when he dilates on the way of repentance and the greatness of God. Some scholars have even found here the summit of the book's message to the sufferer. But Elihu errs, no less than the friends, in the application of his doctrine to the case of Job, and like them therefore merits God's anger in the Epilogue.

With this assessment of the Elihu episode one might compare the treatments offered by R. Gordis in his commentary and B.S. Childs in his *Introduction to the O.T. as Scripture* (London: SCM Press, 1979, 526–44). Gordis (p. 541) accepts that the episode is a later insertion, but attributes it to the same author in old age. The author, he suggests, now has a number of thoughts on suffering to add and does so through the introduction of a new character, Elihu. In particular he teaches here that suffering may be sent to warn someone and turn him back from a fatal course of action (pp. 540–53).

Childs also does not dispute the secondary nature of the episode, but considers what force it would have for a community that accepted the whole book as authoritative. From this angle he sees the Elihu speeches as a kind of commentary on the speeches of God, usefully spelling out the implications of God's somewhat enigmatic appearance.

4. The two speeches of God

God's addresses to Job from the tempest (chs 38–41) are indeed surprising in their subject matter. The descriptions of nature and the animals illustrate the work of God as beyond human comprehension, but there is no treatment of Job's situation or of the operation of justice in the world. That there is no indictment against Job that would justify his afflictions is highly significant, but it is only implied by silence on the matter. More obvious is the implication in God's questions that Job has taken too much upon himself: his 'words without knowledge' have obscured God's purposes. Yet in the Epilogue God will say to the friends: 'You have not spoken concerning me truth as my servant Job has'.

To regard both poetic speeches of God, because of these surprising features, as later additions to the book would be over-hasty. The work would seem very incomplete without the appearance and speech of God to Job. Job's great urge to find God is rightly answered. That it is not answered in the way he or we might have expected can be seen as a mark of the author's insight into the sovereign freedom of God. That our author allows the simple verdict of the Epilogue to stand so paradoxically can also be seen as a stroke of genius. Job had to experience God in his sovereign majesty and mystery and in this be abased; but in the point of his difference with the friends there must be no doubt as to God's verdict.

The question may still be raised as to whether God's second speech is a later addition or an alternative to the first speech. The sharp beginning of the second address (40.6f.) may seem inappropriate after Job's submission (40.3–5). However, the repetition of the whole experience of confrontation and submission is not in itself an unlikely feature; we recall that Pharaoh's dream went over the same ground twice for its better confirmation (Gen. 41.32).

The second speech admittedly differs in character from the first in several respects. The challenging questions are not nearly so pervasive. Instead of short presentations of numerous phenomena we have long accounts of only two. And what on earth are these? They are certainly somewhat remote from experience, whether we hold to their mythical character or their similarity to the African hippopotamus and crocodile (or with some scholars, the elephant, whale or dolphin). It is all rather different from the well-observed phenomena of the first speech.

On the other hand, the poetic quality remains excellent and the language shows no great difference from the first speech and the dialogue. It may be best, therefore, to regard the second speech as intended by the original poet to repeat and reinforce the main effect of God's first speech: a different kind of topic and treatment would be used for variety and development. It is difficult for us to judge how an ancient audience would react to the presentations of Behemoth and Leviathan, but we could imagine that these passages developed the aspect of mystery and marvel. That they are generally less challenging, and are even entertaining, may be an asset in showing that this mighty God is not confronting Job in crushing power. The ending, with no moral drawn (41.34), may be taken as another stroke of genius: God is not here to lecture Job in the manner of an Elihu. We note that Job's second response (42.1–6) is a new expression of his submission, going significantly further than his first.

5. Appreciating a complex and expanded work

Our discussion of the growth and structure of the book may help us the better to appreciate *Job* as a work of varied parts, joined together with some tensions, and yet all the more powerful for that.

The original work of the great author, as we have seen, can be taken to have comprehended the Prologue, Job's lamenting curse, the three rounds of speeches with the friends, Job's concluding statement, God's two speeches from the storm with Job's two responses, and the Epilogue. The third round of speeches may well have been more complete and consistent than it is now, but we cannot be sure how to reconstruct it. The poem on Wisdom lies rather outside the dramatic movement and may have been included later, as being from the same circle and broadly relevant. The episode of Elihu stands out very clearly as a later addition by someone of inferior skill and unable to share the insight of the original author.

The original work already had its inner tensions. The author exploited the contrasts between the traditional tale and his dramatic speeches. When the passive Job becomes the fighting Job, everyone must sit up! So simply, so tellingly, the dogmatists, who often sound so right, are brought down with a mighty fall at the last moment. Job is in the end both abased and exalted. The theory of rewards and punishments is battered, yet Job is finally heaped with blessings. Here were contrasts, tensions and surprises enough to give those who experienced the great author's work a good jolting and the chance of rare enlightenment.

The inclusion of the poem on Wisdom added something to the paradoxes. For here Job already seems to know what he has to learn later. The audience perhaps reflects at this point on the swings of mood in a sufferer, and on the difference between teaching and direct encounter with God.

When the work includes the Elihu episode, the suspense and fluctuation increase. The audience must wonder what to make of this confident new speaker, who means to put everybody to rights. Some may at once discern that, for all his fresh efforts, he, no less than the friends, is on the wrong tack and will only make greater the fall of Job's opponents. Others may catch his enthusiasm and feel it all needed saying: Job's impious words must be thoroughly refuted. Perhaps Elihu's outbursts give them patience to endure the otherwise shocking work, and perhaps the Epilogue in time will do its work and help them to kneel with Job's friends.

In discussing the structure of the work, we have tried to appreciate the interplay of the rather varied sections, and to assess the overall effect at the several stages of growth. Some scholars, especially fifty or a hundred years ago, were so bent on reconstructing the work of the great poet that they discussed each passage chiefly from the point of view of whether it should be 'retained' or 'rejected'. In addition to some of the major sections, they might 'reject' other smaller passages, such as the description of the ostrich. Along with their rejection of various chapters and verses, they would re-arrange the remainder wherever logic seemed to guide them. But no two scholars would arrive at the same original.

Much of the reasoning which they used is good and continues to benefit present students. But with the passage of time their efforts have seemed to be in need of balancing with other considerations. In our discussions we have not thought in terms of deleting or rejecting any passage. We have recognized stages of growth and we have tried to appreciate each one. And it is as well to have only a modest expectation of what our reasonings about growth can achieve. It is better to look patiently for the merits of the present work, rather than rush in to make it seem more logical, for then we should be in danger of simply writing our own *Job*. It is not a question of defending traditional scripture to the last ditch; integrity of scholarship, free from doctrinal prejudice, is essential and to be prized as much as Job, with God's support, prized his integrity. But it is a question of understanding limitations, and, to this end, of benefiting from the history of scholarship.

Of the many theories of the book's development, which together must virtually exhaust every possibility, readers may care to evaluate for example the clear-cut proposal of N.H. Snaith's *The Book of Job: its origin and purpose* (London: SCM Press, 1968). He argues that the author issued his work in three editions. The first comprised the tale and some poetry, including Job's soliloquy and God's answer. The second edition incorporated the dialogue with the friends, and the third introduced Elihu.

6. The poet and his audience

In trying to appreciate the work in its growth and complexity, we may find it helpful to imagine the way in which it was presented to a public. Nothing is actually known of this, but the nature of the work and of the ancient society leads us to certain probabilities.

The form of *Job* is ideally suited to dramatic recitation or presentation. A narrative sets the scene with a vivid prologue; a few characters exchange long and lively speeches in poetry, leading to a climax and its resolution; the narrator rounds off with an epilogue. The sim-

plest presentation we could imagine would be where one reciter, originally the author himself, declaimed the whole work, using gesture
and voice-colouring to bring the succession of characters to life. But
it is interesting that the Prologue and Epilogue take care of all the
action that would be elaborate to perform as a drama, leaving just the
simple interplay of poetic speeches. This arrangement could be delib-
erately made to facilitate a rudimentary drama and encourages us to
imagine that along with the narrator there were reciters for each role.
That one of the reciters should convey speeches of God would not
seem strange in a society that knew the custom of prophecy. For such
a production all that would be required would be a narrator and six
reciters, a 'place of spectators' (the Hebrew of 34.26b may be so
translated) such as a threshing floor or a gateway, and, most important, an audience with a taste for poetry.

Kinds of drama had long existed in the sacred festivals of the Near
East (see e.g. H. Frankfort, *Kingship and the Gods*, Chicago: Chicago
University Press, 1948, 123–39; J.H. Eaton, *The Psalms Come Alive*,
Oxford: Mowbrays, 1984, 116–44, 155–56). In Greece in the sixth
and fifth centuries BC we find tragedies with very little action and few
roles developing from the lyrical recitals of a single actor supported
by a chorus (see *The Oxford Classical Dictionary*, ed. N.G.L. Ham-
mond, Oxford: Clarendon Press 1970, 630, 1083–88).

In pre-Islamic Arabia, with a population that may have had much
in common with Job's 'tribesmen of the East', appreciation of recited
poetry was highly developed. 'When there appeared a poet in a family
of the Arabs, the other tribes would gather to them and wish them joy
of their good luck. Feasts would be prepared, the women would join
together in bands, playing upon lutes as they would at weddings, and
the men and boys would congratulate one another' (Ibn Rashiq; see
C.J. Lyall, *Translations of Ancient Arabian Poetry*, London: Williams
and Norgate, 1930, xvii).

A traditional item in the Arabian poems was a description of animals of the wild. Creatures such as the wild ass, ostrich, eagle, hawk,
camel and horse were depicted with expert knowledge. The audience
relished also other scenes of nature, such as the desert storms, and
precepts of proverbial wisdom (Lyall, xix, xxvi). Composition, recital and preservation were accomplished through the ancient oral
methods. Every poet had his *rawi*, 'reciter', to whose memory he
committed his poem, and who in time passed it on to others. Chains
of such tradition are known to extend over centuries. The *rawi* not

only knew the master's text, but also had knowledge to explain its allusions or difficulties (Lyall xxvf.). With the rise of Islam, poets were at first in disfavour. But once, an outlawed poet contrived to be allowed to recite before Muhammad. His recitation, though entirely in the old secular style, nevertheless so moved the Prophet that he threw his own mantle to him as a gift (C. Brockelmann, *History of the Islamic Peoples*, London: Routledge and Kegan Paul, 1949, 33–34).

We can likewise imagine that *Job* also was declaimed from memory with the relishing of every syllable, evoking fascination with the suspense and resolution of its drama. In its history of recitals, it would be likely to develop to some extent in response to its audience, as European works of theatre and concert-hall have often done. The beauty and general relevance of the poem on Wisdom would make it a welcome addition, and the audience might enjoy additions to the list of curious animals, for example the ostrich. A time might come when adverse reaction, perhaps from a new ruler, prompted expansion with the Elihu episode. It is interesting that care was taken to incorporate this criticism of Job into the dramatic form, with the creation of a new role. Dramatic recital of the work may thus have still been customary.

Artists and public help each other and lift each other to high standards. How a poet can speak when his listeners 'wait eagerly as for the rain and open wide their mouths as for spring showers' (29.23)! A society which appreciated hearing great poetry was answered by a tradition of great poetry, and *Job* survives as its great example. As we strive to appreciate it in its parts and in its whole, in its earlier and late forms, we join a succession of rapt audiences. Like them, we must listen with open and eager mind, allowing our imagination to be stirred, our sympathies engaged. We meet the happy Job, the shocked and tormented Job, the clumsy and indignant counsellors, the arrogant know-all, the God in the storm with his pictures of skies and seas and animals, the new Job and his dear Jemimah, Keziah and Keren-Happuch. Sometimes we can sit with the audience which heard a shorter *Job*, sometimes with those who heard it with expansions. In either case, there can be rich reward, as the poet leads us to a seeing with our very own eyes.

7. Theme in the Prologue

Let us now gather our observations regarding the leading ideas in the various parts of the book. The Prologue, we found, was designed above all to prepare a situation where the most righteous servant of God was subject to the worst possible misfortunes. A situation is thus prepared where the poet can explore how the sufferer and his friends will view this crisis. The details of how the situation is set up are therefore subservient to the main aim, and in fact the issue between the Lord and the Satan is never referred to again. Even so, the idea is of considerable interest: 'Does Job fear God for nothing?' Is his reverence of God disinterested, or is it practised in order to gain the advantages of riches and security?

Under the surface of the crudely child-like story lies a profound question: do men love good, or love God, *purely*, for the sake of what they love? Or does self-interest turn even their best loves into a form of self-seeking? And if it were found that the servant whom God estimated to be his best served the giver for the sake of the gifts, would it not be a condemnation of God himself, as well as of the whole human race? So, unknown to himself, Job will go out naked into the darkness as the champion of all goodness.

We can also observe that the Prologue sets out a framework of thought and faith for the whole work in beginning from a world ruled by one God, upholder of order and justice. An event is launched which will seem on earth to be in conflict with justice, but it is not anarchical; there is good purpose in it.

8. Theme in the Dialogue

Following upon their journey to visit their stricken friend and their commendable sitting with him for a week in silence, the friends of Job between them make eight animated speeches. Commendable also is their desire to help Job find restoration (contrast 34.36). They claim that their point of view rests upon traditional wisdom received from generations of fathers and supported by fresh revelations (4.12ff.; 8.8ff.; 15.7ff.). And indeed, their teaching is similar to passages in Proverbs and Psalms.

They stress that God rules the world with supreme power, wisdom and justice, bringing retribution upon the wicked, who also suffer continually from apprehension before the blow falls. But he is ready to forgive those who repent. When calamity begins to strike, then, the wise man will at once heed the warning, forsake his sins and turn to God in humble penitence. God will even give him several warnings if he is slow to respond. The truly wicked man is he who hardens his heart, as though scoffing at God's correction. For him full retribution is certain. Job's stand seems to the friends to be near this final wickedness. His refusal to see his ordeal as just retribution for well-concealed sins reminds them of the brazen scoffer; he appears to reject the hallowed teaching of God's justice and they are outraged. What human being can have the confidence in his own righteousness to dispute the evident verdict of God? He finds faults in the heavenly beings, let alone in our sin-prone race!

The ethical standards of the friends are not reflected as fully as Job's but are no doubt similar. They see the wicked man as defiant and callous towards God (15.25ff.). He crushes and abandons the poor or seizes their homes (20.19). He takes the last stitch from the destitute as bail, withholds bread and water from the needy, adds to his lands by force, is harsh to widows and fatherless (22.6ff.). Such are the ideas of the men who in the end will have to rely on Job's prayers to save them from God's wrath! It is not surprising that our author met some misunderstanding, resulting in the Elihu episode and perhaps the changes in the third cycle of the dialogue.

What he has shown is how men acting with good intentions and hallowed ideas can fall into gross error. In the interests of their doctrine, they have preferred falsehood to truth; they have misrepresented the wider scene of human fates, and have abandoned faith in their old friend in favour of baseless accusations, wounding further the stricken and lonely sufferer.

While the friends uphold the justice of God by sacrificing truth, Job, no less a believer in divine justice, is plunged into a tremendous conflict by holding to truth at all costs. Provoked by the friends' doctrinaire descriptions of a world where just retribution everywhere takes effect, he points with realism to conditions of misery and injustice in the world, where no divine power protects the weak, oppressors flourish unchecked, and death in the end is the same for good and bad.

Job will not shift the responsibility to some satanic power. God alone is responsible (9.24), just as the attacks upon Job himself are taken to be direct attacks of God (16.7–14; 19.6–22). It is to God, then, that Job appeals, and he frequently leaves off disputing with his friends to make appeal to God. In spite of his bitter realism about actual conditions, his appeals assume a framework of justice. If God has cause against him, let him show Job his error (10.2; 13.23) and forgive him (7.21)! If there has been a miscarriage of justice, may Job have the chance to defend himself at God's tribunal! Here apprehension rises that he would not to be able to make his defence against so mighty an adversary (9.13–35). But through all his fears and bewilderment, his strongest conviction is that he will find justice; the false accusations will be swept aside and God himself will take his part (13.13ff; 16.18–17.3; 19.23ff.; 23.3ff.; 31.35).

So in spite of his direct experience of inexplicable calamity and of his open recognition of injustice rampant in the world, Job holds to his faith in God's goodness. Even his bitterest laments draw their force from this sense of the just and true and from his recognition of God as the all-powerful and only one. His underlying conviction of the justice and fidelity of God goes with remembrance of the loving care of God his personal creator (10.8ff.; 29). It is this background of experience and conviction that makes the present savage attacks so dreadful.

Job's struggle is all the more poignant because of the sense of the brevity of human life and finality of death. Feeling himself very near to death, he recalls how brief is human life before it passes irrevocably into an extinguishing darkness. All the problems of injustice seem the more acute with this universal fate near at hand (17.14ff.; 21.21ff.). Most touching is his thought that if only man, like a tree, could revive from death, he would gladly wait in the darkness till God, longing for the creature his own hands had made, should call him forth, and each would answer the other in friendship (14.7–17). But more than touching is his thought that God will appear as his 'redeemer'. For here is a bed-rock of conviction. Let death and all its darkness come; God will establish the truth and clear Job's name, and somehow Job will know that God *is* his faithful friend and will be satisfied (19.23ff.)

This is not a doctrine of resurrection. But such a conviction of God's ultimate fidelity, maintained along with Job's utter realism about earthly life and death, is infinitely precious.

The ethical ideas of such a man of truth and integrity are of special interest. They are eloquently expressed in chs 29–31. The good man lives in the sense of God's reality. He knows that the light leading him through darkness comes from the lamp of God above his head. The righteousness which clothes him is a matter of generous and brave action for the poor. His faith and courage are a support for the many who despair. Conscious of God's penetrating knowledge, he obliges his eyes not to lead him to sin against the young girls who could be in his power. He is not enticed into adultery. He is steadfast against corruption and fraud and the secret sins of the hypocrite. He listens fairly to grievances of his servants, shares his bread with the needy, clothes the naked, respects the rights of the weak, does not worship gold or sun and moon, acts well towards his enemy, is a generous host, lodges the wayfarer, seizes no lands nor schemes against their owners.

The ethical precepts here are drawn from tradition. The ideal of hospitality seems to be especially exalted in the lands fringing the desert and is well represented, for example, in the stories of the semi-nomadic patriarchs (Gen. 18.2–8). The care of the weak and needy is a fundamental teaching in the main near eastern societies earlier than Israel. Deeply rooted in Israel was the claim of their God to be worshipped alone, and to be respected as defender of the oppressed and the lord of all concerns in life (Ex. 20–23). Even Job's remarkable restraint towards his enemy has its parallel in the traditions of laws and proverbs (Ex. 23.4–5; Prov. 24.17–18). (A discussion of the forms and ethical traditions affecting this chapter is given in English by G. Fohrer, 'The righteous man in Job 31', *Studien zum Buche Hiob*, 78–93.)

Job's statement, then, is impressive not for novelty, but for its selection, motivation and eloquent passion. Here is a vivid apprehension of life in the light of God, the one God who is the maker and guardian of that person who has come into our path. Notable also is the confidence that the ideals are attainable. The author knew the argument that man could not be righteous before God (4.17), but his drama turns upon the integrity of Job, recognized by God himself (1.8) and here brought to its most courageous expression. It would therefore be inappropriate to regard Job's avowal as marred by a self-righteousness from which he must later 'repent' (42.6).

In the poem on Wisdom (ch. 28), man is portrayed as the great searcher. At the limits of his sphere he digs and probes, searches and researches for what is precious; from darkness under the earth, from the sources of springs, he wins treasure of fine stones and metals. But that which is beyond the price of all such treasure he cannot reach and grasp; the wisdom that the Creator alone has, he can never wrest into his hands. But there is still a good way for him: to listen to the word of God which teaches him to fear God and reject evil.

9. Theme in Elihu's speeches

Elihu's confidence rests on his claim to be inspired rather than on the teachings of the fathers. He reckons that since God, as all-wise and all-powerful, must be in the right, a creature in opposition to him must be in the wrong. One who speaks critically of God's rule of the world is a scoffer. Elihu, by contrast, gives an unrealistic account of how divine justice is ever manifest in the world. Men's afflictions are warnings from God to evoke repentance. There are angels, too, who help the sinner to repent and find forgiveness. So relief comes, and happy thanksgiving at the sanctuary. But are there not many who cry out and are not delivered? Their cries, in that case, are not genuine prayers which recognize God as their maker and saviour. It is for man, then, to submit to God and to praise him as wise beyond all our comprehension, as his works in nature show.

Elihu takes further the friends' arguments by more closely considering the experience of repentance. He distinguishes instinctive cries for help from the prayer of faith. Against the critics of God, he advocates the praise of God, whereby man acknowledges God's infinite superiority.

These speeches, we have seen, may have been added to make up what was thought to be lacking in the defence of reverent piety. Points from the speeches of the friends and of the Lord are elaborated in harsh and confident criticism of Job. But it is difficult to see the speeches as in fact strengthening the positive teaching of the book. Rather they seem to demonstrate still further how hard it is for many people to sympathize with the innocent sufferer and how hard to contemplate truthfully situations which conflict with prior doctrines. All the more precious is the Old Testament's testimony that God himself will hear the outspoken lamentations of a Job, a Moses, a Jeremiah or a Habakkuk, and will appreciate that, for all their bitterness, they speak in truth.

10. Theme in God's speeches

It would be interesting to know how we should have composed these speeches if we had known only the preceding chapters. At all events, the speeches may surprise us in making no reference whatever to Job's sufferings. There are neither words of comfort nor accusations. The majesty of God is present. Through the questions and the pictures of nature Job experiences the godhead with a directness which supplants the need to argue and criticize. So neither party raises the issues which have filled the preceding controversies. The meeting is thus not at all as Job expected. The divine is ever surprising. It evokes in him no terror nor a cowed, confused mind, but wonder, self-abasement and peace.

Almost all the material of God's speeches (the exception is 40.11–13) is illustration of his work in nature—creation, phenomena of weather, animals (mostly in the wild). It is not the magnitude and sheer power which are brought out, but joy, beauty, care, and above all, wonder—the very springs of worship. The ironical questions establish the proper proportions of the divine and the human in the encounter. But they do not have the harshness which rings through the Elihu speeches. A humorous note seems to grow stronger, and as the second speech progresses the questions give way to entertaining and absorbing portrayals of mysterious monsters. The fierce conflicts of the preceding drama move to resolution in the face to face meeting of God and his faithful servant.

The paradoxes of faith and experience are not explained. Argument fades away. Job held to the truth and now, still in the darkness and bereft of all human comfort, he is granted a revelation of God which surpasses every other experience. In this revelation a major part is played by the artist's vision of beauty. The voice of God comes almost exclusively in scenes of nature, finely observed with the artist's eye, beautifully expressed in the poet's words. These matchless speeches represent God as the divine craftsman, artist and poet; from his work human art and faith must catch their vision.

11. Theme in the Epilogue

There is much to ponder in the childlike story of the Epilogue. If there were surprises in God's appearing to Job, his address to Eliphaz amounts to a shock. Eliphaz, who has cited a heavenly voice to reinforce his admonition to Job, now hears God's voice without qualification declaring him wrong. He and his companions have not spoken what is real concerning God, as Job has. They must humbly beg Job to intercede for them, lest God fall on them in unrestrained anger. After the criticisms of Job in the eight speeches of the friends, in four speeches of Elihu and (implicitly) in two speeches of God, this is the first word in his favour. Brief as it is, it is utterly decisive.

Yet Job seemed to speak near-blasphemy, and the friends spoke so reverently! Job, however, showed his belief in God by committing himself to the truth, while the friends, in not trusting the truth, revealed their unbelief. Doctrinaires all of them, the friends looked for safety in a lie, and thereby offended against their stricken friend and no less, it now appears, against God.

It is remarkable that God himself gives directions for intercession, naming the person by whom he will let himself be restrained (cf. Gen. 20.7f.). The simple narrative here takes up the great mystery of the power of prayer, and ascribes to it a key place in the working of God's grace—by the appointment of God himself. The intercessor is chosen in advance by God, a righteous man, a man of faith and truth and, as it happens, a man in the greatest suffering and loneliness, rejected by his society.

For Eliphaz and his friends there is the humiliation of having to ask this man, whom they have condemned as ungodly, to pray for their forgiveness by God. For Job there is the challenge first to forgive them their slanders. He evidently does so in a good spirit.

And it is when Job has prayed for his erring friends that God restores him with a great salvation. Here too there is much food for thought. Throughout his long lamentations, he has necessarily dwelt chiefly on his own ordeal. The speeches of God surprised by ignoring it. Job is forced by God's questioning to centre his attention on the majesty and wisdom of God, conveyed in the beautiful vignettes of skies and seas and storms and wild beasts. And then, in victory, his attention is turned to the need of his friends. His forgiving love and prayer come first. Only after that come the healing and open vindication of Job. So the self-absorption which acute problems wrap around the sufferer is cast off. He sees reality that does not centre on himself and his own perplexity. Such a release is linked by our story with the wonderful restoration of Job.

The restoration disappoints some readers of Job. They feel it savours too much of the traditional doctrine that the righteous man is never forsaken; his troubles may be many, but in the end all comes right for him (cf. Ps. 37.24ff.). And so, they feel, it has fallen below the great poet's standard of realism as attained in Job's speeches. But a story is not a dogma. The book does not lay down the way in which God must always act to show his faithfulness to his suffering servants. It shows how in the present case that faithfulness was suitably manifested. Before the eyes of all his society Job was vindicated, as the story required. For Job had followed a path which enraged all the religious pundits, and God now gave his approval to Job in a language they would understand.

The Epilogue is eloquent also in its silences. As in the poetic speeches of God, so here there is no reference to the heavenly council of the Prologue; nor is the reason for Job's ordeal disclosed. This is in harmony with the book's discrediting of those who claimed to explain Job's suffering. The story has told of a great suffering for which there was a reason in God's purpose, but not a reason known on earth. So the last word is not given to anarchy in human fates, however anarchical things seem. But for man there remains the inexplicable. He has to suffer in the dark and keep faith when all the waves of chaos roll over him.

12. Theme in the Book of Job

We have seen that the parts of the book all have their own eloquence. Each has its own particular themes which elsewhere in the book may appear scarcely or not at all. But what can we say of the theme of the book as a whole, the 'purpose' of the book, the fundamental concerns which prompted its creation?

The author has built his work on the story of a supremely righteous man who suffered appalling and unmerited calamities. Hence his theme deals with the contradictions in our experience of 'God', the power beyond ourselves, the reality that makes and governs the world; God as good and yet apparently cruel; just and faithful and yet apparently indifferent to justice. In the experience of Job the clash of creation and chaos is intensely represented: creation producing order, beauty, truth, goodness; chaos surging back in moral anarchy and senseless human destinies. From his story the author does not propound a general explanation of this conflict; he offers no intellectual solution of 'the problem of evil'—such would indeed be a betrayal of the experience he is exploring.

His story does not deny the ultimate supremacy of the good. Job's fate is not shown as the product of blind forces. In spite of all that points to the contrary, his world is in the hands of the good Creator. But the human experience of all that seems to belie God's goodness is represented most frankly in Job's speeches. Job suffers without any knowledge of the divine purpose. He speaks of God attacking him savagely and unjustly. He is horrified to think that he who created and led him with every appearance of love should have been all the while intending such cruelties against him. From his own situation he perceives without illusion the extent of injustice in all the world—the oppression of the poor and the impartiality of death.

But the poet's theme now rises to its climax. He shows this Job openly facing the universal evil, and yet, in his deepest convictions, believing in truth. Job's faith appears no longer in the formulas of a well-drilled piety. Rather, his faith is evident in his refusal of the attractive but dishonest course advocated by the friends; it is evident in his continuing appeals to God; and it is evident above all in those great resurgences of confidence in his ultimate vindication. Of all that he knows of God, the sweet and the bitter, it is the justice and fidelity which will have the last word; such is the conviction which is wrested in blood and tears from his ordeals.

The final manifestation of God to him and the verdict of the Epilogue, with all their unexpected features, serve above all to confirm Job's costly insights. The theme of the book can thus be recognized not as a theory of the problem of evil, but as the portrayal of a man who knew the problem in all its horror at first hand, and yet, without a trace of dishonesty or illusion, staked his life on goodness: 'Though he may slay me, I will hope in him' (13.15). Faith without dishonesty or illusion, faith that wins in the teeth of savage and senseless chaos— such is the theme of our book.

The friends are a foil to this portrayal of Job. Here are men who have a ready explanation of the contradictions of faith. Here are men who draw on traditional teachings and even on their mystical experience to buttress their comfortable piety; men whose theology hardens them to dishonesty and the slandering of a stricken friend. This was the danger which our author felt it necessary to combat, rather than the danger of 'scoffing', cynicism about the rule of a moral God—a point of view which he has not felt moved to embody in any of his characters.

The confirmation of Job's insights is reached with his abasement before the manifest God, and it is publicly clarified in the Epilogue. Noticeable in God's speeches is the absence of discussion of the problem of evil: not even to Job's ordeal is there any reference. God is revealed to Job as inexplicable, transcendent in wisdom and power, but certainly the good Creator, who cares for his works, and for beauty, truth and order. It is a revelation of the Holy One which evokes wonder and self-renouncing adoration. It is confirmation enough of

Job's faith in ultimate order and truth, and so brings utter satisfaction. Vanished are Job's notions that the sufferings expressed God's hostility or blame; vanished his criticism of God's dealings with mankind. All such bitter outpourings he renounces as he rests content in the presence of the Creator.

The author's theme thus carries him into the heart of religion, into the heart indeed of all human experience which wrestles with the contradictions of hope and despair, light and darkness, creation and chaos. He follows his theme through with rare insight, sensitivity and originality, yielding a treatment which can scarcely be surpassed.

This crucial question of the book's main theme is answered variously by modern writers, but with a certain convergence on the issue of faith and relationship to God.

G.B. Gray wrote a closely-argued account of the purpose of the author in the Commentary by Driver and Gray, pp. l–lxiv. It is rather an intellectual interpretation, concluding that 'the book aims not at solving the entire problem of suffering, but at vindicating God and the latent worth of human nature against certain conclusions drawn from a partial observation of life' (p. li).

A concise and cogent treatment of the book's theme is given by H.H. Rowley, *From Moses to Qumran* (London: Lutterworth, 1963, 141–83). Comparing Paul's experience of God's power 'made perfect in weakness' (2 Corinthians 12.8f.), he finds that the author of *Job* was above all interested in the miracle of profit wrested from suffering through the enrichment of the fellowship of God.

Pope, in his Commentary (pp. llxviiif.), considers that the greatest question faced is, how can men put their faith in One who is the Slayer of all? Faith in him cannot be achieved without moral and spiritual agony, and it is founded in despair of reliance on lesser causes.

A particular view of the theme of the book arises from the form-critical study of C. Westermann, *The Structure of the Book of Job* (Philadelphia: Fortress Press, 1981; original German 1956). The element of 'lament', he says, is fundamental. The sufferer is not concerned to debate, but to call for God, and God in the end comes.

3

QUESTIONS
OF CONTEXT
AND LANGUAGE

1. Comparable literature

IT IS EXTREMELY interesting to compare *Job* with treatments of the problem of suffering in other ancient cultures. As we examine the texts which happen to have survived, the distinctive splendour of *Job* is in no way diminished; but it becomes clear how early and widespread was the struggle to retain a moral explanation of experience. In various particulars, too, we find similarity to *Job*—in the poetry of lament and hymn, in proverbial wisdom, in dialogue form, in certain themes of argument. There is little or no cause to suppose a direct dependence of *Job* on any of the non-Israelite works. But placing *Job* in the context of the wider human questioning cannot but enlarge our understanding.

From the Sumerians, and hence from the third or early second millennium, comes the *Lamentation to a man's god* (Pritchard, 589–91; for this and the following references see Note on Sources at the end of this section). This is a poem which teaches the sufferer to persevere in calling upon his god with praise, lament and confession of sin (for the sages teach that all men are sinners). After a brief exhortation to such praise and lament, the poem introduces a man who, though of good life, was overwhelmed with sufferings. His lamentations are quoted at length, and the poem ends by describing how his god at last heard him and turned his sorrow into joy. This teaching is similar to that of Job's counsellors, but the poem does not underestimate the bitterness of the ordeal. The exemplary sufferer complains to his god that his righteous words have been overwhelmed by the lies of his friends, while his god does nothing to help, but rather deals out to him ever more troubles. Why should he be treated as the wicked? How can his god neglect one like his own child? Supported by mourning women (family and professional) he depicts his weeping and how the demons of sickness bathe in his body. It seems that the bitterness of the complaint was at least as important as the concluding brief confession and entreaty in securing the help of the god.

Three texts from the Babylonian literature of about the later second millennium deserve close attention. *I will praise the Lord of Wisdom* (Pritchard, 596–600; Lambert, 21–62) is the thanksgiving of a ruler, a moi ologue praising the supreme god, Marduk, and narrating how the ruler suffered, lamented and was delivered. Within the framework of praise, the recollection of the suffering and the lament is again very bitter. The ruler complained of being forsaken by his divine protectors, thrown down from his social eminence, forsaken by family and friends and exhausted by disease, his bones protruding and falling apart. His fate was like that of the ungodly, whereas he had lived piously. It seemed that the gods reversed the values, despising the good and liking what should be despicable. Who could understand them? He was appalled at the paradoxes of experience. There was no answer from his god; the diviners could tell him nothing. His tomb was ready. But this dark passage ends with what seems to be an invincible confidence that justice would prevail:

> But I know the day for all my family,
> when, amidst my friends,
> their sun-god will have mercy.

This is in some degree comparable with Job 19.25.

He goes on to tell of dreams which signified that Marduk's wrath was appeased and that he would now deliver him. So Marduk restored him part by part, driving away maladies and transgressions. Healed, he made procession to Marduk's temple, declaring himself an example for all who transgressed the requirements of that temple. Let them see how Marduk in his mercy restores to life! If Tablet IV is the proper continuation of this composition, the concluding praises of Marduk's universal rule and the account of the procession through eleven symbolic gates and of the offerings are especially fine. In any case, we have here a text which on the one hand recognizes the inscrutable nature of the divine wrath, but on the other holds to the way of faith and praise.

The Babylonian Theodicy (Pritchard, 601–14; Lambert, 63–91), a sufferer's dialogue with his friend, is an acrostic poem of twenty seven stanzas, each of eleven lines. The dialogue form, which runs

from beginning to end, serves to express the difference between the
reality of suffering and the traditional pious teaching on the subject, a
sharp difference not concealed by the studied politeness of the two
speakers. The sufferer relates his troubles to his friend, who attempts
to restrain his bitterness, recommending prayer and just conduct and
warning against the madness of the reckless questioner. Examples of
retribution in nature and society are considered. The sufferer
deduces that those who neglect the god prosper, while those who pray
are made destitute. The friend declares this to be blasphemy, doing
away with propriety and the divine order; one has to accept that the
god's plans are hard to grasp, the divine mind remote.

Pressing on with examples of justice going awry, the sufferer
depicts how people will bear false witness to support the rich against
the poor. The friend acknowledges this and explains that the gods
gave man a lying nature at his creation. Thus the friend, upholder of
piety, concedes the gods' responsibility for wrongs in society, and so
the sufferer's complaint is unappeased. He ends with an appeal for
pity from his friend and mercy from his guardian spirits, affirming
that the sun-god (god of justice) is shepherd of the peoples. In this
last line we may find more than a formal clinging to hope in divine
justice against all appearances; it is in accord with the sentence
formed by the poem's acrostic, where the author of this unspoken
work declares that he is one who reverences the god and the king.

The third Babylonian text, *The Dialogue of Pessimism* (Pritchard,
600–601; Lambert, 139–49), is also a dialogue throughout. The
speakers, a master and his servant, seem to be characterized satiri-
cally (the compliant servant, the rich idler), but the underlying
theme, the enigma of human existence, is serious enough. Each time
the master announces to his servant what he proposes to do, the servant promptly affirms the advantages of the proposal. The master at
once decides against it, and the servant as promptly affirms its disad-
vantages. Outings in the chariot, dining, marrying, loving a woman,
sacrificing, acting against or for the benefit of society—all courses are
considered and rejected. On the ancient ruin-heaps the skulls of good
and bad cannot be told apart. So what is good? Suicide? It is all
beyond puny man's comprehension.

In this brilliant little piece, the dramatic form enables the author to
speak through his characters, leaving the audience to make of it what
they will. Here is a rich young man who could have done anything,
and is reduced to nothing. And here is a slave, superior in ability,

ironically deferential, a pessimistic philosopher. His ready switches of advice serve to air the commonplace palliatives before confronting them with a bitter reality.

From Egypt of around 2000 BC come two striking texts. In *The Dispute over Suicide* (Pritchard 405–407) a man relates a dialogue he has held with his soul; in the central section his speech runs without interruption through four symmetrical poems. The subject is his desire to commit suicide, burning himself like a sacrifice. Sickened by life on earth, he is positively attracted by the hope of life after death, which on the Egyptian view might be a higher life with the gods. He already calls upon the gods who judge the dead to judge and defend him aright. But his soul is cautious. If even kings could not be sure that their tombs and funerary rites would be maintained, how much less a man of modest means! A poor labourer cannot expect a meal in the afternoon as well as in the evening, and likewise the man should not look for relief before his proper time.

The soul's prudence provokes the man into his four passionate poems. The theme of the first is 'My name will reek through you', i.e. 'You disgust me'. The theme of the second is 'To whom can I speak today?'—the wicked flourish, the gentle have perished; there is no friendship, and the sin that treads the earth has no end. The theme of the third is 'Death is in my sight today as . . .'—as all that is lovely: like healing, like cool air, like scent of myrrh or lotus blossom, like coming home from captivity. The theme of the fourth is 'Surely, he who is yonder will be . . .'—a living god, travelling in the barque of the sun, a sage who can commune with the great god Re. This eloquence affects the soul, who ceases to object and promises to make his home with the man after death.

The second Egyptian text is *The Protests of the Eloquent Peasant* (Pritchard, 407–10). It is a story in prose, though within the story the peasant's nine speeches on justice have a semi-poetic eloquence. The peasant had been wronged by a vassal of the Chief Steward. He reported the matter to this great official, whose advisers made light of the case. The peasant thereupon made his first eloquent speech, extolling the blessings of the ruler who is the father of the orphan, the husband of the widow, the brother of the divorcee, and the apron of the motherless. The Chief Steward was so impressed that he told the Pharaoh about the peasant's eloquence. The Pharaoh accordingly arranged that justice should be long delayed, so that the peasant would have cause to make further eloquent expositions of justice which were to be recorded and sent to the Pharaoh for his delight. Meanwhile provision was to be made for the peasant and his family without the source being disclosed.

So the peasant had to make eight further appeals, all proving to be of the same high standard, though for one which roundly condemned the Chief Steward he was whipped. At the last, when he was expecting death and welcoming it as water to the thirsty and milk to the babe, the Chief Steward raised him to honour and gave him the goods of his oppressor. The story does not call in question the justice of the gods. They are indeed its upholders, and it is for their sake that a man must do justice, which will accompany him into eternity and secure him a name for ever on earth. But students of *Job* will note especially this mysteriously protracted ordeal of a man who continued to appeal for justice and would have preferred to die rather than give in to unjust force.

Job's affirmation of innocence (ch. 31) is sometimes compared with the Egyptian mortuary texts collected by modern scholars into a 'Book of the Dead' (Pritchard, 34–36). In this material the dead person is imagined as posthumously affirming before a court of gods his innocence of various sins, including adultery, lying, stealing, murder, fraud, mistreatment of animals, and blasphemy. Sometimes there are positive claims: 'I have given bread to the hungry, water to the thirsty, clothing to the naked, and a boat to one who was marooned'. These texts witness to a long ethical tradition, but are not especially close in form and topic to Job's affirmation.

Before leaving Egypt we may note that some ground common to Egyptian and Israelite Wisdom teaching may underlie the great speech of Job 38–39. There are two features of the speech which may (as von Rad has argued) owe something to materials and methods of such teaching, namely the list of natural phenomena and the style of questioning. The *Onomasticon* of Amenope (published by A. Gardiner) lists all that the Creator (Ptah) made in heaven and on earth and coincides occasionally with the order of items in *Job*. In the *Satirical Letter of Hori* (Pritchard, 475–79) an official seems to adopt the teacher's method of closely questioning his pupil and aims to deflate a scribe who has written to him. On the subject of geography he plies him in lofty and sarcastic manner with some fifty questions, which must have been enough to make him feel his ignorance.

From north Syria of the second millennium comes the Ugaritic legend of *Keret* (Pritchard, 142–49; Gibson, 82–102), a good king who had much to suffer. Seven times he had married and each time the wife died childless. His position as king was becoming untenable. Crushed, he lamented to heaven, his tears streaming to the ground like shekels. The god El, father of mankind, was moved to help him and guided him through various adventures to secure the right wife. She bore him eight sons and eight daughters, and the youngest daughter was endowed with the birthright of a first-born. But Keret was humiliated again: having failed to fulfil a vow to the goddess, he was smitten by a grievous sickness. His wife rallied his people to lamentation and sacrifice on his behalf and he was miraculously restored, just in time to ward off his son's attempt to replace him. The story shows an expectation that suffering lies near at hand, even for the most venerable of mankind, in this case a king regarded as the intimate of El. Twice he is crushed, to be restored only when lamentation moves El to intervene.

Of the famous Greek dramas which explore the tragedies of life, *Prometheus Bound* by Aeschylus most rewards our attention. Thought to date from the end of the productive author's life and so from c. 457 BC, it is but the first of a trilogy. The lost sequels will have provided the resolution of the conflict, as can be judged from surviving fragments, from prophecies in the first play, and from the well-known myth which Aeschylus adapted.

With the help of this myth he was able to carry the complexities of experience back into the divine order. Zeus has violently supplanted the earlier generation of gods and rules the universe tyrannically—harsh, lustful, a law to himself. Prometheus, from that earlier generation, had first supported him, but then had earned his wrath for standing up for mankind. The play opens with the punishment of Prometheus. The servants of Zeus are clamping and skewering him to the mountains at the edge of the world. Kratos ('Power') cynically urges the others on, while the victim preserves an impressive silence. Only when they leave him does he break into pathetic and indignant soliloquy.

After this prologue, the body of the play contains no action but conversation between this motionless 'crucified' and a series of visitors. The Chorus enters first; these daughters of the god of the ocean are to stay with him till the end. They are sympathetic, but rather shocked by his uninhibited defiance of Zeus, and they counsel restraint. Good advice comes easily from the spectators of suffering, comments Prometheus! But he is sure that one day Zeus will want reconciliation and will eagerly seek him as a friend. The conversation serves to fill in the background of the story, and Prometheus recalls how he had helped mankind by giving them blind hope to veil the inevitability of death, and fire from which came many crafts; he introduced thought into their work, teaching them counting, writing, transport on land and sea, medicines, mining.

The ocean god himself makes a brief appearance. His professions of friendship, coupled with advice to placate Zeus, only stir Prometheus to sarcasm: 'You're such a help! One thing I'll always admire in you—you're never short of good intentions!' Another visitor is the girl Io, victim of the desire of Zeus and the jealousy of his consort goddess, and so driven in torment across the world. Through her the sufferings of humanity and gods are linked, and it will be a descendant of her union with Zeus, Herakles, who will free Prometheus.

The last visitor is Hermes, messenger from Zeus. Prometheus has spoken of a secret he possesses, his last card to play against Zeus. Defiantly he has threatened his tormentor with it. He knows of a future spouse of Zeus through whom will come his downfall. Hermes has been sent to demand the facts, so that the danger can be averted. Prometheus will not yield, though foreseeing the rage of Zeus. Hermes warns the gentle Chorus to leave the place of danger, but they prefer to stay and suffer with Prometheus rather than condone his treatment. The play ends with Prometheus depicting the shattering descent of the furious Zeus and calling on earth and heaven to behold the wrongs he suffers.

The play exposes the evils of the world, and especially the overwhelming ruthless violence, which, however, cannot silence the protests of reason and pity. The lost sequels will have filled out the prophecies of Prometheus. With the passing of ages the situation would evolve. Other aspects of Zeus would appear. Prometheus would be persuaded to reconciliation for the sake of all, including mankind. The world's torment passes at last into harmony and joy.

It is interesting that this drama has so little action on stage. Between the fastening of Prometheus and the finale conjured up by his last speech, the motionless chief actor simply converses with the Chorus and a succession of three visitors. The drama is in the development of ideas and attitudes. From the changes of metre we can trace the three kinds of delivery: speech, chant like recitative accompanied by instruments, and song accompanied by instruments. The spectacle would be enhanced by the dancing of the Chorus.

From India comes a notable treatment of suffering in the legend of King Haris-candra. One version appears in a Sanskrit text, the *Markandeya Purana*, Cantos VII–VIII. Jaimine, a seeker of instruction, is told the story by four learned birds of marvellous origin. The tale unfolds in speeches of the characters, alternating with the narrating speeches of the birds, and so approaches dramatic form. It tells of righteousness carried to heroic extremes, thereby entailing horrific degradations until at last the gods appear.

Vighna-raj, a spirit who is 'the opponent of every undertaking', wishes to frustrate a powerful brahman (Visvamitra) and contrives to make him angry with the righteous king Haris-candra. The harsh ascetic takes advantage of the king's heroic piety to take from him all his power and possessions, reducing him and his wife and son to abject poverty. As the oppression continues, with many a pathetic turn, the royal couple are about to immolate themselves, when the gods Dharma and Indra show themselves. It turns out that in the king's final humiliations as servant in the hideous place for burning corpses, his repulsive employer has been Dharma in disguise. The gods reward the king with bliss in heaven, which he only accepts when he is granted the same bliss also for all his people. He has argued that a king does great deeds of piety only through the influence of his citizens, and so these humble benefactors must share out his reward, even if this leaves him with but a day of bliss. The piety of Haris-candra continues to benefit all who in suffering learn from his patience and devotion to truth and goodness.

The story lives on in various forms of recital and dance, and summaries appearing in our biblical text-books can make it seem quite similar to Job, especially when beginning with a scene of gods planning the king's ordeals. But an article by David Clines, a splendid piece of detective work, ('In search of the Indian Job', *Vetus Testamentum* 33, 1983, 398–418) shows that these accounts, borrowed from one to another, must be treated with caution. Even when they accurately reflect Indian oral sources, it is difficult to know what details are ancient and independent of biblical influence. It would be hazardous, then, to use this story in the quest for the sources of Job. The interest of this very Indian legend is rather in its own insights into the hidden meanings of experience, the cost of righteousness, the value of humility, and the interdependence of the seekers of good.

Finally, comparisons within the Hebrew Bible must not be forgotten. Although *Job* as a whole is unique here, there are many parallels for the form and ideas of particular passages. *Job*'s background in the traditional teaching of the sages can be illustrated from Proverbs, where ch. 3, to take but one example, includes the themes of God's just dealings, his chastening of those he loves, and his creation of the world by wisdom. One whole work from this tradition, Ecclesiastes, is in its way as challenging as *Job* in its penetrating honesty.

The struggles of Israel's thinkers to understand harsh experience are represented also in the Psalms. The counsel of trust and patience is given in Psalm 37, while testimony to relief and a saving enlightenment is found in Psalm 73. Psalms of praise share with *Job* the portrayal of God as Creator and sustainer of the world, of man and all that lives (e.g. Pss. 8; 33; 104; 139). The numerous lamenting psalms (e.g. 38; 39; 69; 86; 88) illustrate the traditional approach of sufferers to God, with many parallels to the lamenting passages in *Job*.

Similar laments occur in the prophetic books and Lamentations. Thus the justice of God is sharply challenged in Habakkuk 1.2–4, 12–17 and in the 'confessions' of Jeremiah. 'Why does the way of the wicked prosper?' asks Jeremiah; God plants them and they spread roots and bear much fruit (Jer. 12.1–2). It is Jeremiah who exceeds Job's bitterness by cursing not only the day of his birth but also the good man who carried the news (Jer. 20.14–18). Malachi hears much bitter complaint from his contemporaries: 'Every doer of evil is pleasing in the eyes of the Lord! Where is the God of justice? Serving God is futile. We may as well call the arrogant blessed' (Mal. 2.17; 3.14–15). Is this bitterness in part a reaction against the insistence of Deuteronomy on God's just punishment and reward of the nation? Is *Job* another example of such reaction? For *Job* at any rate, the comparisons we have been making in wider literature suggest this theory is unnecessary.

For the narrative art of *Job*'s prologue and epilogue we could especially compare the idyllic Ruth and the stories of the Patriarchs (e.g. Gen. 24). Israelite narrative knew much of human adversity, and every generation must be awed at the sufferings of Jacob, Joseph, Moses, Saul and David.

But in all our work of comparison, within Israel and beyond, we must beware of superficial judgments. Each work must be appreciated as a whole and in its own context. As our interest in *Job* leads us further afield to discover the reflections of many peoples, we can only gain through enlargement of sympathy and so return to *Job* with all the more understanding and admiration.

Note on sources and further reading

The following are the sources referred to above:

J.B. Pritchard (ed.), *Ancient Near Eastern Texts relating to the O.T.*, Princeton: the University Press, 3rd edn, 1969. (A fine collection of translated texts with short introductions and notes. Earlier editions can be used with addition of the Supplement, *The Ancient Near East: Supplementary Texts and Pictures*, 1969.)

W.G. Lambert, *Babylonian Wisdom Literature*, London: Oxford University Press, 1960. (A full edition of original texts with translations, introductions and notes. Since this edition and Pritchard's, more lines of 'I will praise the Lord of Wisdom' have been recovered, making it all the clearer that praise of the god is a recital telling alternately of his kindness and his harshness; see D.J. Wiseman, 'A new text of the Babylonian Poem of the Righteous Sufferer', *Anatolian Studies* 30, 1980, 102–107; W.L. Moran, 'Notes on the Hymn to Marduk...', *Journal of the American Oriental Society* 103, 1983, 255–60.)

G. von Rad, 'Job 38 and ancient Egyptian Wisdom', in his *The Problem of the Hexateuch and other essays*, Edinburgh and London: Oliver and Boyd, 1966, 281–91.

A.H. Gardiner, *Ancient Egyptian Onomastica*, London: Oxford University Press, 1947.

J.C.L. Gibson, *Canaanite Myths and Legends*, Edinburgh: T. & T. Clark, 2nd edn, 1978.

The Markandeya Purana, translated by F. Eden Pargiter, Calcutta: The Asiatic Society, 1904, reprinted Delhi: Indological Bookhouse, 1969, 32–58.

Aeschylus, *The Prometheus Bound*, ed. G. Thomson, London: Cambridge University Press, 1932, reprinted New York: Arno Press, 1979. (Excellent introduction, Greek text, facing metrical translation, and notes.)

Aeschylus, *Prometheus Bound*, translated by J. Scully and C.J. Herington, London: Oxford University Press, 1975. (Introduction, translation into idiomatic modern poetry, glossary, and a good appendix of the translated fragments of the sequels.)

D.J. Conacher, *Aeschylus' Prometheus Bound, A Literary Commentary*, Toronto: Toronto University Press, 1980.

Other useful collections of translated texts:

W. Beyerlin (ed.), *Near Eastern Religious Texts relating to the O.T.*, London, SCM Press, 1978.
D. Winton Thomas (ed.), *Documents from O.T. Times*, London: Nelson, 1958, New York: Harper, 1965.

General works on Wisdom:

J. Blenkinsopp, *Wisdom and Law in the O.T.*, London: Oxford University Press, 1983.
J.L. Crenshaw, *O.T. Wisdom: An Introduction*, London: SCM Press, 1981.
G. von Rad, *Wisdom in Israel*, London: SCM Press, 1972.

2. Poetry and language

Since *Job* is most widely known through the transforming medium of translation, some comments on the character of the original poetry and the qualities of the standard translations may be helpful.

The easiest feature to recognize in the Hebrew poetry is parallelism, where a short statement is repeated in other words or balanced in some other way:

> May my enemy fare like the wicked
>   and my attacker like the perverted! (27.7)

> But where can Wisdom be found,
>   yes, where is the home of Understanding? (28.12)

Each of these verses can be thought of as a 'line' made up of two balancing 'members'. These members in *Job* usually contain only three Hebrew words or word-groups, giving a rhythm of three stresses to balance with three in the parallel member. It is hard to see any rigid rule about the number of syllables or exactly what is allowable as a word-group, but the system has several obvious qualities. The wording of the clause in Hebrew is very lean; elaboration takes place in the addition of the balancing clauses, which uses many subtle variations. The whole line of two (occasionally three) members can itself be balanced by following lines, and such extended parallelism is much exploited in the cumulative eloquence of *Job*. Chapter 29, for example, can be seen throughout as a beautiful unfolding of the opening line:

> Oh that I were as in months long passed,
> as in days when God guarded me! (29.2)

Sometimes an idea remains the same in several lines:

> Eyes I was to the blind,
> yes, feet to the lame was I,
> Father was I to the poor,
> the grievance of a stranger I examined,
> And I broke the fangs of the cruel,
> yes, from his teeth I freed the prey. (29.15–17)

And sometimes the thought is moved on with a line beginning 'when' (29.3) or 'because' (29.12) or 'then' (29.18).

With this method of short, balancing clauses there is a fundamental simplicity of utterance, but also the opportunity to extend into large patterns of rising eloquence. It is like the short, bold brush strokes of van Gogh, which dance together into a whole living scene. (Patterns in groups of lines are studied by E.C. Webster, 'Strophic patterns in Job 3–28', *Journal for the Study of the O.T.* 26, 1983, 33–60.)

Our poet speaks through traditions of great antiquity, which reach back beyond Hebrew to the beginnings of Near Eastern literature. There is the ancient style of proverbs (e.g. 8.11–13; 11.12; 12.5, 11, 12; 17.5; 24.19). The ideas and phrases of the lamenting psalms are used extensively (e.g. 7; 14; 30.16–31). The language of the hymns depicting God's works, especially in creation, influences many passages (e.g. 9.5–10; 26.6–14; 36.24–33; 37). We catch the style of the examining teacher (38–39) and the rhetoric of public speech and dispute (8.1–2; 11.2–3; 15.2–3; 21.2, 3, 5; 33. 1–5; 34.2–3; 38.3). Through such stock of traditional utterance our poet is yet able to create poetry of outstanding freshness and power.

The imagery of *Job* remains fairly clear in translation, though one may need to take account of cultural and climatic conditions to feel its force. Many images are noted or explained in our 'Reading' above, such as the sparks (5.7), curdling milk (10.10), the sprouting stump (14.7–9), archers (16.13), the grim home and family of death (17.13–14), dancing lambs (21.11), miners (28), the weight of the wind and the measure of the waters (28.25), God's lamp (29.3), rivers of curds and oil (29.6), words like rain-drops (29.22–23). How vivid the scene at the gate (29.7–25), how menacing the gang of scavengers (30.1–15)!

Our poet excels in the speeches of God. He shows us the eyelids of the dawn (41.18, also 3.9), the swaddling band of the sea (38.9), the coverlet of the sleeping earth (38.13); the horizon at dawn like the impressing of a seal (38.14), the home from which God daily leads out the light and darkness (38.19–20), the heavenly stores of snow and hail (38.22), God who binds the stars in clusters (38.31) and tilts his waterskins to give rain (38.37). He paints for us the lion, the raven, the calving hind, the wild ass and ox, the ostrich, the war-horse, the hawk and the eagle (ch. 39), and primeval beasts more marvellous than the hippopotamus and crocodile (chs 40–41).

Job contains many words that are rare or unique in the Hebrew Bible. Some of these are better known in the sister language Aramaic, while explanations for many difficult words can often be attempted from Arabic. These peculiarities may be largely due to our poet's command of the resources of Hebrew, ranging across the dialects. It could possibly point to his origins on the eastern or southern fringes of Hebrew areas, where the language would have more Aramaic and Arabic colouring. It is questionable that it points to a late date, when Hebrew was giving way to Aramaic in Palestine, since there is nothing deficient in our author's Hebrew. Aramaic had only gradually become distinct from the Canaanite group to which Hebrew belongs, and its special colour can be noticed here and there in Hebrew literature of all periods.

The use of the names of God in *Job* is noteworthy. 'Yahweh' ('the Lord') and 'Elohim' ('God') are used in the prose passages (Prologue, Epilogue, and lines introducing speakers), whereas in the poetic speeches 'El', 'Eloah' (both rendered 'God'), 'Shadday' ('The Almighty') and more rarely 'Elohim' are used. To this distribution there is only one exception, when 'Yahweh' occurs in the stock phrase of 12.9. The readiest explanation of the usage is that the author was a worshipper of Yahweh, writing for such, but in the poetic speeches, which were peculiarly his creation, he preferred the patriarchal usage for its archaic atmosphere. The use of 'Yahweh' in Job's mouth in 1.21 may reflect the traditional wording of the story.

We are well served with English versions. The Authorized or King James Version, beloved as English literature, had less resources than recent versions to tackle the difficult Hebrew vocabulary (it has, for example 'unicorns' in 39.9–12 and 'peacocks' in 39.13). But it passes on some of its music to two great revisions, the Revised Version of 1884, which is invaluable for its close reflection of the Hebrew wording and for its cross-references, and the Revised Standard Version of

1952, which generally avoids antiquated English and draws on modern knowledge. Of the new translations (as distinct from revisions) the New English Bible of 1970 has much to offer both in style and philological insight. If it be thought too bold in emendation (e.g. 19.26) or in re-ordering the text (e.g. chs 24; 31), a subsequent conservative treatment in modern English can be found in the New International Version (1978). Also in modern idiom, and prepared to emend and re-order, is the Jerusalem Bible (1966), deriving from the scholarship of the French Dominicans; it is much valued for its fine production and notes. For simple clarity the Good News Bible (1976) is winning popularity; its resort to simplifying paraphrase (e.g. 28.28; 31.10) is well thought out, if a little hazardous.

3. Date and circle of origin

There are only broad considerations to help ascertain the date of *Job*'s composition. Opinions have varied from a Jewish belief in Moses' authorship to the view of critics who, supposing Plato's influence, look to Hellenistic times. If we confine ourselves more realistically to the period of mature achievements in Hebrew language and thought, we could still range from the tenth to the early fifth centuries BC.

Most theories rely on showing relation with other Hebrew works. There is some value in this type of argument, though it must be remembered that it is not always clear in which direction an influence has passed, and that two similar texts may be drawing independently from a third, or indeed from a long tradition. Advocates of the seventh century can make some relation with Jeremiah, Habakkuk, Deuteronomy. The sixth century may be claimed especially with reference to the comparable eloquence of Isaiah 40–55 (e.g. in Isa. 40.12–31). An early fifth century dating would fall conveniently between Zechariah (where 'the Satan' appears, Zech. 3.1–5) and Malachi's defence of God's justice; here too, some argue, the Persian empire would give conditions for international experience and for Aramaic influence on Hebrew. If these considerations are hardly compelling, still less is the proposal to see Job as reflecting the fate of Israel in exile and restoration.

Job's homeland, Uz, is connected by one tradition with the Hauran, east of Galilee, perhaps because Genesis 10.23 lists 'Uz' as son of 'Aram' (= Syria). Other biblical texts point to the region of Edom, south-east of the Dead Sea, especially Lamentations 4.21.

Some scholars (e.g. Pfeiffer) therefore see the author himself as an Edomite, especially as the wisdom of Edom is mentioned in Obadiah 8. Others locate him beyond the border in Arabia. Explanations of rare words in *Job* are often based on comparison with Arabic, and A. Guillaume found the Arabic influence so strong that he supposed the author was resident in a Jewish colony in Arabia. He connected the attacks of the Sabeans and Chaldeans in Job 1.13–17 with Babylonian campaigns in Arabia and asserted that *Job* must have been written in the Hijaz in the latter part of the sixth century (*Studies in the Book of Job*, Leiden: Brill, 1968, 7–14).

But all that we can confidently conclude from the evidence used in all these proposals of date and provenance is that the author was able to set his work in a region bordering the Syro-Arabian desert, and that he commanded wide resources of the Hebrew language. Whatever connexion he might have had with Syria, Edom or Arabia, he stands in the theological tradition of the Israelite worship of Yahweh, the sole God though attended by heavenly beings, the Creator who has allotted man his life-span on this earth only. He was at home in the open intellectual tradition we call 'Wisdom', in the rhetoric of dispute, and in the psalm language of lament and praise. He lived in a circle where poetic art was highly developed and appreciated, especially through the medium of oral and dramatic presentation. While comparisons with extant Hebrew literature may seem to favour a date between the seventh and fifth centuries, our comparisons with two millennia of non-Israelite texts warn us to keep an open mind.

4. Landmarks in the reading of Job

Let us finally see *Job* in the context of the literature it has evoked, though we mention but a small sample. An exciting discovery among the Dead Sea Scrolls was a targum of *Job*—a translation (with very slight explications) into Aramaic, the language of Jesus. The rather fragmentary manuscript dates from the first century AD and the rendering will have been made perhaps a century earlier. There are many points of interest here, such as the understanding of 42.6 as 'Therefore I am poured out and dissolved and become dust and ashes'. The fragments extend from 17.14 to 42.11, where the manuscript seems to have ended. It is published with introduction and facing French translation by J. van der Ploeg and A. van der Woude (*Le Targum de*

Job de la Grotte XI de Qumran, Leiden: Brill, 1971). The existence of this very early targum suggests a keen feeling for the importance of the book. From Jewish tradition we have also remnants of a midrash (a kind of homiletic exposition), and there are valuable mediaeval commentaries, such as that of Ralbag (see Bibliography in the commentary of Gordis).

From the sixth century comes an exposition of *Job* in thirty-five books by Pope Gregory the Great; his Latin text, originally delivered as practical homilies to monks in Constantinople, is being published with a facing French translation (Grégoire le Grand, *Morales sur Job*, Sources Chrétiennes, Paris: Éditions du Cerf, from 1950). Calvin's hundred and fifty-nine substantial sermons on Job are highly esteemed ('the greatest exposition of *Job* ever given'—F.I. Andersen). Twenty are selected and translated by Leroy Nixon, with an introductory essay by Harold Dekker (*Sermons from Job*, Grand Rapids, Michigan: Eerdmans, 1952; Baker Book House, 1979).

A remarkable pictorial interpretation is given in William Blake's *Illustrations of the Book of Job* (London, 1825). How well he expresses the thought that God's poetic speeches create the scenes they describe and rivet the attention of Job and his wife, who gaze up to see the singing stars of the morning and down to see the monstrous beasts in the depths! Job's pilgrimage is towards the ascendancy of imagination and art (see J. Beer, *Blake's Visionary Universe*, Manchester: Manchester University Press, 1969, 269–73).

Modern study of Job centred first on the composition of the book—what passages might be later interpolations etc. The main lines of the debate are already clear in S.R. Driver's *Introduction to the Literature of the O.T.* (Edinburgh: T. & T. Clark, 8th edition, 1909, 408–35). Comparisons with R.H. Pfeiffer's *Introduction to the O.T.* (London: Black, 1952, 660–707) shows how the debate intensified. The situation was not unlike that of classical studies described by G. Thomson: 'The weakness of their method was that, in considering what those poems had been, or might have been, they failed to consider what they were' (*The Prometheus Bound*, 38). But in an intellectual crisis early in this century, *Job* spoke powerfully of 'the numinous', the holy Presence that evokes awe and transcending peace (R. Otto, *The Idea of the Holy*, ch. 10, London: Oxford University Press, 1968; original German 1917).

In the eloquent work of E.G. Kraeling, *The Book of the Ways of God* (London: SPCK, 1938), we see re-emerging the desire for broa-

der appreciation and a role for the imagination. Two small studies
had outstanding quality: H. Wheeler Robinson, *The Cross of Job*,
1916, revised 1937, then reprinted in *The Cross in the O.T.* (London:
SCM Press, 1954), and T.H. Robinson, *Job and his Friends* (London:
SCM Press, 1954). Good commentaries were not lacking, as noted at
the outset of our study. C.G. Jung's wide-ranging reflections in his
Answer to Job (London: Routledge and Kegan Paul, 1954, 1979) are
an important example of his blend of psycho-analysis and philosophy
and will long continue to be studied.

In most recent times the appreciation of *Job* as a whole has been
attempted in line with modern literary movements. We are invited to
consider the total effect in terms of comedy, irony, provocative
drama, as in the essays of W. Whedbee and L. Alonso Schökel in
Semeia 7 (*Studies in the Book of Job*, edited by R. Polzin and D.
Robertson, Missoula: Scholars Press, 1977).

Alonso Schökel is one of twelve contributors to an interesting issue
of *Concilium* devoted to Job: *Job and the Silence of God* (Edinburgh:
T. & T. Clark; New York: Seabury Press, No. 169, 1983). The wide-
ranging topics, furnished with bibliography, include 'The figure of
Job in the liturgy', 'Ernst Bloch and Job's rebellion', 'The cry of
Jesus on the cross', 'The people of El Salvador: the communal sufferings of Job', and 'Job in literature' (outlining a 'Joban' area in imagin-
ative French literature). B.S. Childs considers the completed book as
scripture in his *Introduction to the O.T. as Scripture* (London: SCM
Press, 1979, 526–44).

Job's challenge to philology has been taken up again and again and
valuable progress has been made, despite the temptation to explain
too much from one field, such as Arabic or Ugaritic. The Hebraist
can gain much help from the commentaries of Driver and Gray, and
of Dhorme, and of Gordis, and he will find much of value in W.B.
Stevenson's *Critical Notes on the Hebrew Text of Job* (Aberdeen:
Aberdeen University Press, 1951), A. Guillaume's *Studies in the Book
of Job* (Leiden: Brill, 1968), A. Blommerde's *Northwest Semitic
Grammar and Job* (Rome: Pontifical Biblical Institute, 1969), and
L.L. Grabbe's *Comparative Philology and the Text of Job: A Study in
Methodology* (Society of Biblical Literature Dissertation Series 34;
Missoula: Scholars Press, 1977). Through all the intricacy of philol-
ogy, the reward is to find a track to a clearer view of the ancient
author's images, a finer hearing of his voice.

INDEX OF SUBJECTS

INDEX OF AUTHORS